The
Island of
Menstruating Men

The
Island of
Menstruating Men
Religion in Wogeo, New Guinea

Ian Hogbin
late of University of Sydney

WAVELAND

PRESS, INC.

Long Grove, Illinois

For information about this book, contact:
Waveland Press, Inc.
4180 IL Route 83, Suite 101
Long Grove, IL 60047-9580
(847) 634-0081
info@waveland.com
www.waveland.com

Contents

Acknowledgments   xi

Preface 1996 by Abraham Rosman   xiii

Foreword by L. L. Langness   xvii

Glossary   1

I. Introduction   6
    Background   6
    Social Structure   17

II. Culture Heroes   27
    The Mythology   28
    Geographical and Technological Myths   30
    Myths and Institutions   34
    Topographical Myths   38
    The Living Heroes   51
    Conclusion   53

III. The Spirit World   55
    The Souls of the Dead   55
    Mask Spirits and Flute Spirits   58
    Village *Lewa*   59
    Village *Nibek*   72

IV. Taboo   82
    Social Relations between Men and Women   86
    Bwaruka   91
    Manivara   94
    The Context of Sexual Pollution   95

V. **Initiation** 100
Ear Piercing 104
Admission to the Club 106
Scarifying the Tongue 114
Incising the Penis 120
Assuming the Adult Headdress 121

VI. **Menstruation and Childbirth** 125
First Menstruation 125
Menstruation Later 136
Childbirth 137

VII. **Illness and Death** 141
The Young and the Old 141
Normal Reaction to Illness 142
Death 144
Yabou 148
The Performance of Sorcery 152
The Inquest 154
Before Death 156
The Ceremonies 158
Burial 161
Mourning Taboos 163

VIII. **Magic** 168
Magic as Control 169
Another Interpretation 171
Types of Magic 174
Analysis of Magic 176
Examples of Magic 181
Infallibility of Magic 186

IX. **Religion and Social Structure** 188
Magic and Leadership 190
Religion and Kinship 191

CONTENTS

vii

X. The Moral System   193

Wogeo Bibliography   197

Index   199

Illustrations

The Territory of Papua and New Guinea (map)   8
The Island of Wogeo (map)   10
The men's club in Dap village   12
Housebuilding   13
Obelisk and surrounding flat stones   14
Preparing stones for the oven   15
Neighbors preparing a meal together on the beach   16
Taro being prepared for a meal   20
The steersman   44
Masks worn by *lewa* monsters   60
The *lewa* monsters dancing   64
Dance preceding the dispatch of the *lewa* monsters   69
The house of the headman Marigum in Dap village   71
Playing the flutes, which represent the voices of the
    nibek monsters   74
Sending the *nibek* monsters back to the spirit world
    after an initiation   80
Parade of the young initiands in Gol village   112
Janggara, one of the two headmen of Gol village   122
Striking the sounding boards (the *nibek's* bone) as the
    pigs arrive for the feast accompanying an initiation 123
Magar   132
Beating the wooden slit-gong to send a message   157
Burying the dead under the house   162

Magic to keep the outrigger float of a canoe firmly
    attached to the booms   179
Love magic   184

Acknowledgments

My original expedition to Wogeo, in 1934, was financed by the Australian National Research Council, and although this body no longer exists, I wish to record my indebtedness to it (the functions are now served by the Australian Academy of Science and the Social Science Research Council of Australia). When fourteen years later I had the opportunity to return to Wogeo, the then Administrator of Papua and New Guinea, Colonel J. K. Murray, placed a trawler at my disposal to take me from the nearest government station and later to call and pick me up. To him also I am under an obligation.

During the first half of the century so little was known about the anthropology of New Guinea that each field worker who went there was forced to select the community for his study more or less at random. So Thurnwald went to the Sepik River in the west, Malinowski to Mailu and the Trobriands in the southeast, Fortune first to neighboring Dobu and then to Manus in the north and the Arapesh towards the Dutch border, Bateson back to the Sepik after a term on New Britain, and Powdermaker to New Ireland in the far east. My own choice of Wogeo in 1934 was based on the advice of a government anthropologist, Mr. E. W. P. Chinnery. It is unlikely that he had seen any of the inhabitants except as wage laborers in European employment, and I have now forgotten the reasons he gave for mentioning the place. I am grateful, nevertheless, for the suggestion, which proved a happy one.

The nearest point for disembarkation from the ship that had brought me from Sydney was Boram, on the stretch of New Guinea coast off which Wogeo lies. Here the plantation owner and his wife, Mr. and Mrs. Tom Ifould, welcomed me with open-hearted hospitality. They readily agreed to deliver me to the island, replenish my stores after the lapse of six months, and send the schooner over again after still another six months to enable me to board the steamer for the voyage home. I was landed on one of the beaches and spent that night and those following in a deserted dwelling in the village nearby. An important ceremony was in progress, and not until a couple of weeks had passed by could I persuade the people to build me a house of my own. To begin with I had to rely for communication on pidgin English, referred to by some writers as Neo-Melanesian, the Western Pacific lingua franca, but as time went on I was able to speak more and more of the vernacular. After some months I became moderately fluent, though my teachers were never satisfied with my grammar.

In preparing the manuscript I derived constant benefit from discussions with colleagues. My particular thanks are due to Dr. L. R. Hiatt and Dr. M. R. Allen for their penetrating criticisms.

                                             IAN HOGBIN

Preface 1996

Abraham Rosman
Barnard College, Columbia University

The Island of Menstruating Men is a lucidly written ethnography about the cultural construction of gender, which informs us not only about gender relations on the island of Wogeo, where men "menstruate" to rid themselves of the accumulation of "bad blood," but also about gender in our own society.

Ian Hogbin was one of the most prominent anthropologists to have conducted field research in Oceania. He carried out ethnographic investigations in a number of different societies in the western Pacific—Guadalcanal, Ontong Java, Malaita and mainland Papua New Guinea. His work on Wogeo is probably his best research, carried out with insight and understanding. In one's mind's eye, one can see Hogbin, who describes playing 78 RPM recordings of the Mozart oboe quartet on a hand-wound, motor driven Victrola while the villagers of Wogeo listened, commented on breathing technique, and compared Leon Goossens to Tafalti, their ritual flautist. The island of Wogeo is visible when one stands on the high bluff looking out to sea at Wewak, on the Papua New Guinea mainland. It is part of the Schouten Island group, named after Willem Cornelisz Schouten, the great Dutch navigator who circumnavigated the globe in 1615–1617, and made this cluster of islands known to the European world.

The people of Wogeo have a saying: men play flutes, women bear infants, which means to them that males and females have their distinctively different though complementary roles. The two sexes need each other to carry out their respective economic roles and to perpetuate society. Sexual intercourse, necessary in order to reproduce in society, is pleasurable, but it also has its harmful effects—bad blood builds up in men and women as a result. Women have a natural way of getting rid of this bad blood by menstruating every month. For men, the task of ridding themselves of bad blood is much more difficult. Since they have no natural means for doing this, they must be taught how to do it through cultural means. Before they can be taught to "menstruate," they must go through male initiation rites, which is where the flutes come in.

During male initiation, the tongues of the initiates are incised and scarified to rid them of their mothers' blood so that they can become adult men and make their tongues supple, so that they will later be able to play the sacred flutes. The sound of the flutes represents the voices of the secret *nibek* spirits, which are called forth to preside at the initiation rites. Though the women hear the flutes—the voices of the spirits—they are prevented from seeing the bamboo flutes or from seeing the ceremonies.

As described in a key Wogeo myth, two women first discovered the bamboo flutes. When they cut holes in the bamboo, the flutes magically played by themselves for the women. But an adolescent boy stole the flutes. This angered the two women, and they renounced the flutes, proclaiming that from then on the flutes would no longer play by themselves. Men would have to go through the painful process of initiation to learn to play the flutes, hence the Wogeo saying "men play flutes, women bear infants."

The theme of the Wogeo myth, in which women originally discovered and owned the secret rituals, which were then stolen from them by men, is, in fact, widespread in this area, and elsewhere in the world.[1] In the nineteenth century, such myths were taken to represent a previous "matriarchal" stage of evolution. Instead, today, we see such myths as statements about gender relations, as is certainly the case in the Wogeo myth.

The construction of gender in Wogeo raises the most debated issue in anthropological studies of gender: that is, the association of females with nature and males with culture. In Wogeo, the flutes play naturally for females, without the need of cultural intervention, just as females get rid of bad blood naturally, and females produce children through the natural process of childbirth. For men, things are more difficult. Men must learn to do these things during the enculturation process. Boys must have their tongues incised in the painful ritual that turns them into men who play the flutes. They must incise their penises while standing knee-deep in the sea, so that the drops of dangerous bad blood will fall harmlessly into the water and become diluted. In the process, of course, men learn to control the sacred rituals and the powers associated with them, from which women are excluded. While women are associated with natural phenomena, men are associated with culturally learned ritual.

Some of the themes found in Wogeo ritual and gender relations are widespread throughout the north coast and Sepik area of Papua New Guinea. In her classic study of the Mountain Arapesh, described in *Sex and Temperament in Three Primitive Societies* (William Morrow, 1935/1971), Margaret Mead reported that the Arapesh had similar ideas of male "menstruation." Other New Guinea societies report symbolic male equivalents to female childbearing. The Abelam, who live not far from the Sepik, grow long yams which are seen as equivalent symbolically to the children which women can bear. Abelam men, who, of course, cannot bear the children necessary for reproducing their patrilineal society, produce the long yams that they paint, decorate with masks, and exchange among themselves. Just as Wogeo men symbolically equate male flute playing with female childbearing, Abelam men equate yam growing with female childbirth. The theme of male ritual compensation for menstruation and childbearing, so clearly documented in Hogbin's *The Island of Menstruating Men*, is a widespread phenomenon, as is the association of women with nature and men with mastery over ritual, and with it the exclusive control of power.

In describing the rituals and ceremonies of Wogeo culture, Ian Hogbin has made still another important contribution. Wogeo has long been known for the masks used in another focal ceremony, the *warabwa*, when the *lewa* spirits are called forth before a great distribution of pigs held at important political occasions, such as when a headman announces his heir. At this ceremony, completely decorated masked dancers are called forth by village headmen to perform. Hogbin's account of these ceremonies enables us to understand the intricate relationship between art, performance, religion, politics, and kinship in this society. Wogeo masks are alive and powerful when the *lewa* spirits appear at a *warabwa* in *The Island of Menstruating Men*. However, when prominently displayed in museums and sold for thousands of dollars in the auction houses, they hang inertly in the galleries as intriguing aesthetic objects.

Human societies all face certain universal problems, and the nature of the relationship between women and men is one of them. The range of responses in different societies to this seems infinitely variable. Wogeo, where males ritually "menstruate" to imitate female menstruation, is certainly among the more intriguing ways of ordering female-male relations. It raises a number of questions: Are Wogeo men jealous of female menstruation? of the female capacity to bear children? Why is menstrual blood considered dangerous? In some societies over the world, menstrual blood is considered harmful and polluting, while other societies consider it to be inoffensive. These questions will make the reader rethink the nature of gender relations in our society—that is, not only the history of gender relations that are to be found in Judeo-Christian traditions, but the fashioning of gender through American history, and the state of gender relations in the various sub-cultures of American culture today. Rereading a classic ethnography like Ian Hogbin's *The Island of Menstruating Men* compels one to return to the bedrock questions of anthropology.

Notes

[1] A very similar myth has been reported for the Mundurucu of the Amazon by Yolanda and Robert Murphy in *Women of the Forest, Second Edition* (Columbia University Press, 1985).

Foreword

Being asked to write this foreword brings me multiple pleasures. First, Professor Hogbin was good to me at a time, several years ago, when he need not have bothered with me at all. That was a kindness students do not always receive—and one they rarely forget.

Second, it is a pleasure to find a book written by someone so obviously in command of both his language and his subject matter. Ian Hogbin's research in the Pacific spans more than forty years. It includes work on Ontong-Java, Guadalcanal, Malaita, and Busama, in addition to the work on Wogeo which forms the basis for this volume. Further, as this book is merely the latest of many, we benefit importantly from the learning experiences of the author which, in this case, have been rich and cumulative.

More importantly, however, this volume demonstrates that ethnological works can be well written without being necessarily subjective, biased, or somehow nonscientific. The difference between humanism and science has never been precise in anthropology and there have always been a few anthropologists who could *write*, as well as add and subtract. Sir James George Frazer was one, Bronislaw Malinowski another. As this work demonstrates, Ian Hogbin is yet another. This is hardly surprising as Malinowski received the anthropological tradition from Frazer, added to it, and transmitted it to Hogbin, who, in his turn and for many years, has been giving generously of it to all of us.

But not only is the book in the tradition of *literate* anthropology, it also deals with the study of religion. This is a subject which was dropped for a time in anthropology, curiously enough, because it was regarded as unscientific; but the interest has been revived in recent years and now it is once again considered a legitimate anthropological pursuit. Thus, as is pointed out in the first chapter this book is the first full-length study of a Melanesian religion to appear since 1935. It examines the question of religion as it relates to many other facets of culture—mythology, beliefs about illness and death, growth and maturity, magic, social structure, and morality. It is an articulate, insightful examination of the meaning of tradition and of the integration of culture. It is also a fascinating account of ethnocentrism and the Wogeo's justification for it, exemplifying, in miniature, what appears to be one of the great problems of the human species.

L. L. Langness

Glossary

The definitions below follow the conventions accepted by most British anthropologists. There is less agreement in America, where a number of terms, for example "clan," are used in several different senses.

Affines (*adj.* affinal). Persons related by marriage, for example a man and his brother's wife, a woman and her husband's brother.

Agnates (*adj.* agnatic). Persons descended in the male line from a common ancestor. The same as patrilineal kin.

Avunculo-virilocal. *See* Residence after marriage.

Bilocal. *See* Residence after marriage.

Bride price, bride wealth. In traditional societies the wealth collected at marriage from the bridegroom's kin and distributed among the bride's kin.

Clan. A unilineal descent group, patrilineal or matrilineal, within which the specific connections with the founding ancestor or ancestress, real or putative, are unknown. Many of the members in consequence are unable to say exactly how they are related to one another. A clan is said to be *localized* when the adults of one sex, or the majority of them, live together in one place, *dispersed* when both sexes live scattered over a wide area. Usually, though not invariably, the clan is exogamous.

Cognates (*adj.* cognatic). Persons descended from a common ancestor or ancestress. The descent may be traced in any way —through males exclusively, through females exclusively, or through males and females indifferently. Thus the cognates include the agnates, the uterine kin, and all the other kin.

1

Corporate group. A recognized body of persons who for some purpose or purposes act together as a single entity. They may hold land or other property jointly, or they may have the responsibility of carrying out blood revenge should one of their number be killed, or they may be obliged to assemble from time to time to carry out a prescribed ceremony, or their appointed leader may be the sole representative in dealings with outsiders. Often the clan and the lineage are corporate groups.

Cross cousins. The children of siblings of opposite sex, that is, of a brother and a sister.

Descent. A relation mediated by a parent between a person and an ancestor, defined as any genealogical predecessor of the grandparental or an earlier generation. A grandparent is thus a person's nearest ancestor. If descent is traced through one line only it is said to be *unilineal—patrilineal* when the line is of males, *matrilineal* when of females. In some places descent is *double unilineal,* that is, traced simultaneously through males for some purposes and through females for other purposes. A minority of British anthropologists insist that the term necessarily implies unilineality, but the majority refer to *nonunilineal* or *cognatic descent* where it is traced through males and females.

Descent group. A kin unit in which descent, unilineal or nonunilineal, is the necessary criterion for recruitment.

Dowry. Wealth that the father presents to his daughter on her marriage. When dowry consists of land, which usually is in the care of the men of the community, its management may be entrusted to the husband; but if divorce occurs the woman retains the property as her own. Dowry is not the reverse of bride price, nor is it a form of "husband price," as is sometimes stated. It is also not to be confused with *trousseau,* the household goods and utensils, usually gifts from her kin, that a bride brings to her new home.

Exogamy (*adj.* exogamous). The rule of marrying out; the insistence that a person must seek his or her spouse from outside a particular social group of which he or she is a member. Often the moiety, the clan, and the lineage are exogamous. It is wrong to speak of a single marriage as exogamous if by chance the husband and wife happen to belong to different groups. The opposite of exogamy is *endogamy,* the rule of marrying in. In a given society one set of groups may be exogamous and simultaneously another set endogamous, for instance where exogamous clans are coupled with endogamous castes.

Filiation. The fact of being the child of a specified parent and hence deriving rights, privileges, or responsibilities from him or her. *Patrifiliation* if the parent concerned is the father, *matrifiliation* if it is the mother.

Incest. Sexual intercourse between persons related in specified prohibited degrees of kinship. The prohibited degrees differ widely from society to society. Within one society marriage and incest prohibitions do not necessarily coincide, and often sexual relations are tolerated between persons who are forbidden to marry.

Inheritance. The transmission, according to recognized principles, of the property of a person, usually deceased, to an heir (or heirs). *Patrilineal inheritance* when it has to go to a son, *matrilineal inheritance* when to a sister's son.

Kin. Two persons are kin when one is descended from the other or when both are descended from a common ancestor or ancestress. Persons are *cognatic kin* or *cognates* when the descent is traced through males, females, or males and females indifferently.

Kindred. A set of a person's cognates recognized for social purposes. A kindred is always centered on a single individual and is reckoned through male and female links. The members of a person's kindred need not be, and often many of them in fact are not, related to one another. In a small community kindreds of different persons, unless they are full siblings, necessarily overlap.

Kinship. Genealogical relationship, real or putative, recognized and made the basis of the regulation of social relations between individuals.

Lineage. A unilineal descent group, patrilineal or matrilineal, within which the specific connections with the founding ancestor or ancestress, real or putative, are known. The members in consequence should be able to say exactly how they are related to one another. Usually the lineage is exogamous.

Matrilateral. On the mother's side. The matrilateral cognates are the kin with whom the mother provides the link.

Matrilineal. In the female line. Matrilineal cognates, or uterine kin, are kinsmen who trace descent from a common ancestress through females.

Matrilocal. *See* Residence after marriage.

Matri-uxorilocal. *See* Residence after marriage.

Moiety organization. A division of the society into two groups, to one of which each person must belong. Often the moiety is a unilineal descent group, patrilineal or matrilineal, and it may also be exogamous. But some societies are divided into halves on the basis of residence, allocation by a constituted authority, or personal choice.

Parallel cousins. The children of siblings of the same sex, that is, of two brothers or two sisters.

Patrilateral. On the father's side. The patrilateral cognates are the kin with whom the father provides the link.

Patrilineal. In the male line. Patrilineal cognates, or agnates, are kinsmen who trace descent from a common ancestor through males.

Patrilocal. *See* Residence after marriage.

Patri-virilocal. *See* Residence after marriage.

Preferred marriage. The preference in any given society for marriage between relatives of a particular category, for example a man and a matrilateral cross cousin. This type of union is not to be confused with *prescribed marriage*, the rule eliminating choice and enjoining marriage between relatives of a particular category.

Residence after marriage. When a couple marries, the woman may leave her kin and join the husband in the dwelling he has built (*virilocal* residence), or he may leave his kin and join the wife in the dwelling her relatives have built (*uxorilocal* residence). These terms have replaced those formerly current, respectively *patrilocal* and *matrilocal*, now mainly used in compounds. *Patri-virilocal* residence is where the couple lives among the husband's patrilineal kin; *avunculo-virilocal* residence, where they live among his matrilineal kin; *matri-uxorilocal* residence, where they live among the wife's matrilineal kin. If the couple alternates between the husband's kin and those of the wife, regularly spending some months with each, residence is said to be *bilocal;* if they move away from their kin to a new place it is said to be *neolocal;* and if they do not set up a common household but continue to live in their respective natal homes it is *duolocal.*

Sibling. Persons of either sex who have the same parents are said to be full siblings; if one parent only is shared they are half siblings; and if a man with a family marries a widow or divorcee with a family, the two sets of children are step siblings.

Succession. The transmission, according to recognized principles, of the office, status, rights, and privileges of a person, usually deceased, to an heir. It is *patrilineal succession* when the office or the like has to go to a son, *matrilineal succession* when to a sister's son, *adelphic succession* when to a brother.

Unilineal. In one line, of males exclusively or of females exclusively.

Uterine kin. Persons descended in the female line from a common ancestress. The same as matrilineal kin.

Uxorilocal. *See* Residence after marriage.

Virilocal. *See* Residence after marriage.

I   Introduction

Early anthropologists were fascinated by the study of religion. Frazer's huge output, for example, was devoted to little else. There were the thirteen volumes of his *The Golden Bough*, the four of *Totemism and Exogamy*, the three of *The Belief in Immortality and the Worship of the Dead*, the three of *Folklore in the Old Testament*, the one of *Psyche's Task*, and more besides. The same might be said of Lang and Marett, though, mercifully, neither was as prolific. The interests of Tylor and Durkheim were wider, but each also saw fit to contribute extensively to the subject.

In about 1920 a change occurred. Religion was not then ignored, but increasing attention came to be paid to such topics as kinship, social structure, economics, law, and politics. Not until thirty-five years had passed did ritual and belief come in once again for intensive treatment. In 1956 the first of a flood of detailed investigations of particular religious systems appeared. Most of the societies concerned were African, and no full account of a Melanesian group has been published since 1935, the date of the first edition of R. F. Fortune's *Manus Religion* (Philadelphia). The present book will, I hope, be the beginning of a series from this part of the world.[1]

Background

Wogeo, located at approximately 3 degrees of south latitude

---

[1] Polynesia is represented by R. Firth's *Work of the Gods in Tikopia*, first edition London, 1940. Mention should also be made of the set of essays by various authors, *Gods, Ghosts, and Men in Melanesia*, edited by P. Lawrence and M. J. Meggitt, Melbourne, 1965.

and 144 degrees of east longitude, is one of the largest of the Schouten Islands (pronounced *Skowten*), which lie some thirty miles off the north coast of Australian New Guinea near the mouth of the Sepik River. The group is not to be confused with another of the same name in the Indonesian territory of West Irian. The neighboring inhabited islands are Koil, Blupblup, Kadovar, and Bam, the last an active volcano in frequent eruption.

The name Wogeo is actually the mainland term; the locals call their home Wageva. Most maps spell it Vokeo, but for this there is no authority. Occasionally it is also referred to as Roissy, the designation bestowed by the Dutch navigators Le Maire and Schouten, who discovered it on July 7, 1616.

The island is about 15 miles in circumference and rises in the center to twin peaks 2000 feet above sea level. It is an extinct, or perhaps only a quiescent, volcano, and there are many hot springs. The core is basalt, but in some parts this is overlaid with areas of breccia, and elsewhere there is a covering of weathered limestone. On the south and east coasts a narrow plain 200 to 300 yards wide intervenes between shingle beaches and the foothills, but in the north and west the slopes begin more abruptly. The soil is rich and the tropical growth prodigious, nourished as it is by a rainfall of some 90 inches. (Records for Wogeo itself are not available, and this is the figure for the nearest government station, Wewak, on the New Guinea mainland.)

There are two main seasons dominated respectively by the southeast trades, from June to September, and the northwest monsoon, from late November to early April. In between, the winds are variable with long stretches of calm. The monsoon period is slightly wetter than that of the trades, but agriculture is not much affected, and planting goes on all the time without a marked monthly rhythm. A calendar permits arrangements for festivals and ceremonies to be made ahead, but the years pass unrecorded, and nobody can tell how old he is.[2]

I spent the whole of 1934 on the island and returned again for a few weeks in 1948. At the earlier date the population was 929 (177 male children and adolescents, 316 male adults, 139 female children

[2]I. Hogbin and P. Lawrence, *Studies in New Guinea Land Tenure* (Sydney 1967), pp. 54-58.

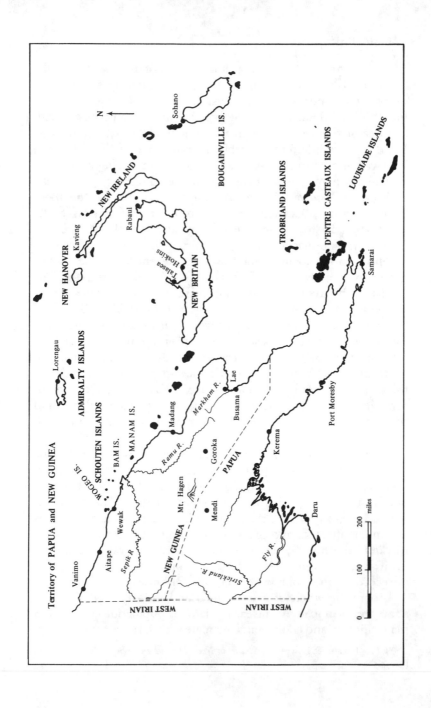

Territory of PAPUA and NEW GUINEA

and adolescents, 297 female adults), but in the interval it dropped by 90 to 839 (112 male children and adolescents, 337 male adults of whom 32 were absent in employment, 76 female children and adolescents, 314 female adults). The fall is probably to be accounted for by introduced venereal disease and lack of medical services, especially during World War II, when for some years the country was occupied by the Japanese.

In appearance the people are typically Melanesian; that is to say, they are Pacific negroids, with dark brown skin, long heads, moderately thick lips, slight prognathism, fuzzy brown or black hair, and clean limbs. Many of the adult men still wear the traditional dress, a hard bark corselet covered with a band of soft beaten bark cloth that passes between the legs and so covers the genitals. The forehead is shaved and the hair pulled back through a wicker cone (*waro*) adorned with cowrie shells and dogs' teeth. The youths reject this cone and, except sometimes on ceremonial occasions, prefer a calico loincloth to the corselet. Females of all ages cling to the clothing of the past. They have a waistband with a series of fringes made from pandanus or sago-palm fiber in the front and at the back. The sides of the buttocks and thighs are bare.

Although recruiters had been taking the young men away to work as wage laborers since about 1905, and the entire group was declared to be under administrative control in 1920, I was the first European resident and possibly even the first European to spend a night ashore. A native catechist of the Roman Catholic Divine Word Mission from Aitape, together with his family, had been landed a couple of weeks before, but he refrained from holding services until late in 1934, and had not established a school when I left in the December. The result was that, apart from the substitution of steel tools for those made from stone, life was going on much as it had been in the precontact era. The social institutions were still functioning according to the old pattern, and although organized raiding and warfare had ceased, murders occurred from time to time. It has to be admitted, however, that of this fact the government was unaware. Official records have nothing to say about killings in 1933 and 1935, or, for that matter, of my presence preventing an outburst of violence in 1934. The intervening decades have brought changes—many of them were already manifest in 1948—but I feel there is justification for my speaking here in the present tense when describing conditions as I observed them.

The natives divide the island into five districts with radial boundaries that follow such natural features as ridges and valleys. At the southeast corner is Wonevaro, and then, traveling in a clockwise direction, come Bagiau, Ga, Bukdi, and Takul. These are grouped into pairs that are traditionally on friendly terms; in addition, each district has a hostile relationship with two others. So Wonevaro collaborates with Bukdi and struggles with Bagiau and Takul, Bagiau collaborates with Takul and struggles with Ga and Wonevaro, and so on.

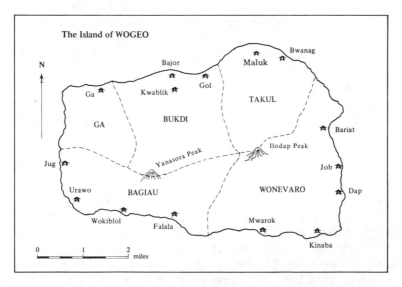

Within each district the component villages are located close to the shore. Bukdi, with the hills descending as cliffs into the sea, is exceptional, and there the settlements—Gol, Bajor, and Kwablik—have had to be built a few hundred yards inland. The majority of the villages have between 60 and 70 inhabitants, though three are only half that size and two, Ga and Bariat, slightly larger.

There are but two schooner anchorages, one off Dap and the other off Mwarok, both in the Wonevaro district. Mwarok is among the smallest of the villages, and I therefore selected Dap as my base. I had a house built just beyond the encircling fence and was soon settled in. The choice proved fortunate. Not only is the place in the center of the region of densest population, but the leader, Marigum, was the most powerful on the island. His son Dal, aged about 17 or 18 in 1934, entered my service, and a sister's son, Jaua, became one of my closest friends.[3]

My original intention had been to spend weeks or months in each of several villages, but events forced me to scrap the idea. For better or worse, I became identified with Wonevaro and hence implicated in the prevailing system of alliances and rivalries. The fact that I was adopted by the Wonevaro residents meant that automatically those of Bukdi received me with a ready welcome. The Gol villagers placed at my disposal a deserted dwelling, which they then repaired, and there I sometimes lived for a couple of weeks; moreover, I developed a warm regard for the two leaders. But the edgy relations of Wonevaro as a whole with Bagiau and Takul, despite the close ties between certain individuals, resulted in my being treated with indifference in these two districts, save when I went to special trouble in creating a personal bond.

In the majority of the villages, the most imposing building, which if the terrain permits stands in the center, is the men's club (*niabwa*). Usually this building is about 20 feet long by 12 feet broad and thus larger than the average dwelling. It is also better put together and has thicker thatch, which projects and so conceals the walls below. The floor rests on stout hardwood piles 8 to 9 feet high, permitting gatherings to be held below. The absence of a club in a few settlements is to be accounted for by the fact that as yet sufficient food has not been accumulated for the feasts that must accompany the construction of a replacement.

The club serves as a meeting ground, a dormitory, and a store for sacred objects. Here the males gather late in the afternoons to

---

[3]Jaua died in 1947, Marigum, after a period during which he was blind, in 1949, and Dal in 1958. Dal's eldest son, Bernie Dal Gagin, born late in 1949, recently (1969) began corresponding with me. He is a student at the Government Teachers' College in Goroka.

The men's club in Dap village.

smoke cigarettes, chew betel, chat, and receive visitors. Sometimes they yell an order to the women to bring the evening meal across. Provided a nocturnal fishing expedition has not been arranged, the younger householders return to the dwelling, but the youths and older men stay on to sleep. The ceremonial objects are lodged on a shelf beneath the rafters. These include flutes, dancing masks, and packages containing the bones of famous ancestors.

Generally the dwellings (*luma*) are in two groups, one at either end of the club. They are of three sizes though identical in design, except that the largest, belonging to headmen, have the walls and gables adorned with paintings and carvings of men, birds, and crocodiles. All are raised off the ground on piles about 3 to 5 feet high and have verandahs in front. The ends are rounded and project to form a shallow apse. The thatch is made from leaflets of the pandanus palm, the walls from the spathes at the base of the leaves of the black palm, and the floors from black palmwood. No nails are used, and everything is lashed in place with cords or creepers. Access is by means of a notched log or a ladder. The apsidal end rooms may be filled with such gear as clay cooking pots, fishing tackle, hunting nets, and extra firewood; or they may be occupied by a widowed kinsman or a married female relative in temporary retreat from her husband after a quarrel. The community leaders live in the largest houses, men with growing families in those of intermediate size, and young or aged couples in the smallest. The collection of building material and the actual construction demand cooperation. The owner of the dwelling being built has to feed the workers and at the end entertain them with a feast, but the principal motive for helping neighbors is not the thought of a free meal but each man's knowledge that the time will come when he also will require assistance.

The father has the obligation of providing the shelter for his family. Where he has several wives, especially if they continually squabble, he may build a separate house for each; or he may relegate the one most open to persuasion to an end room. But as a rule each woman is satisfied with her own part of a single dwelling, and here she cooks at her own fireplace and sleeps with her small sons and unmarried daughters. She may have visits from close relatives of either sex, but her distant male kinsmen never enter unless the husband is present and invites them inside. Usu-

Housebuilding.

ally he prefers to take them to the club. He is supposed to treat his spouses alike and to distribute his attentions equally, but often the last acquired is for the time being the favorite.

Obelisk and surrounding flat stones, all representing culture heroes.—A giant taro rests against the obelisk.

Both men and women avoid the area to the rear of the club, where objects prepared for ceremonies are disposed of afterwards, and the members of each sex group also keep away from the place reserved for the other as a latrine. In theory the different sections of the shore belong to particular sets of relatives, but in practice people pass freely from one to the other and beach their canoes according to convenience. In very hot weather dinner is prepared, cooked, and eaten near the water.

Before the dwelling of every villager of importance stands a columnar block of basalt from a foot to two feet high, and around it several flat pieces of the same stone are embedded in the ground.

Each of these stones is associated with a culture hero with whom the householder claims a special relationship. Indeed, it is this bond that gives him the right to the building site.

The islanders derive the greater part of their daily subsistence from horticulture, and their main implement is still the digging stick, though steel axes and knives were eagerly accepted from the beginning. The slash-and-burn method is employed, and after only a single harvest the ground must be allowed to lie fallow for over a decade before it regains its fertility. Taro (*Colocasia esculenta*) is the staple, with yams, sugar cane, many varieties of bananas, and numerous greens as subsidiaries. In time of feasting, giant taro (*Alocasia macrorrhija*), which grows wild, may be gathered to provide extra stocks, and also quantities of sago may be prepared. The fruits include breadfruit, South Seas apples (*Eugenia malaccenis*), mangoes, and such comparatively recent introductions as the papaya and the orange. Then there are about ten kinds of nuts of which the most important are the coconut, the Canarium almond, a nut with a tough purple husk (*Terminalia kaerndachii*), and the Tahitian chestnut (*Inocarpus edulis*). Cultivated drug plants are tobacco, areca nut, and a pepper creeper, the last two of which are ingredients in the betelnut mixture.

Preparing stones for the oven

Neighbors preparing a meal together on the beach.

Animal protein is derived from fish and pork. Fishing is practiced by every conceivable method—with spears, using a thrower; with line and hook or lure; and with nets. Pigs are kept but are killed only on ceremonial occasions, never to supplement the everyday diet. Hunting expeditions for domestic animals that have escaped to the hills and have bred there are also organized from time to time, but it would probably be correct to say that, spread over the year, the average intake of meat is not more than a couple of ounces daily, and perhaps less.

Cooking is carried out by roasting directly on the fire, steaming or boiling in a clay pot, or baking in the familiar Pacific-islands oven. For the oven, stones are heated till they are red hot. Then half are removed and laid round a depression in the ground, a light covering of leaves goes on top, then the food, next another thin covering of leaves, the rest of the hot stones, and finally a thick pad of leaves weighted at the edges. The oven is always used for pork and when a crowd of guests is being entertained.

Voyages between Wogeo and Koil are fairly frequent, and occasionally intermarriage takes place, but contacts with the other Schouten Islands and with the mainland are sporadic. A fleet of some half-dozen overseas canoes is fitted out in Wogeo every five or six years and sets sail for trade with a series of island villages and others on the New Guinea coast. On the outward voyage the vessels carry the local specialities—Canarium almonds and certain other nuts—together with fishing nets and small woven baskets. These goods are exchanged for such objects as clay pots, large bags for the women to use for carrying garden produce (they suspend them from a strap passing over the crown of the head), pipeclay to serve as a cosmetic, bamboos to be fashioned into flutes, and such ornaments as shell rings, cowrie shells, bird-of-paradise skins, and the plumes of the Victoria crowned pigeon (*Goura victoria*). After the lapse of two or three years the mainlanders reciprocate and in their turn arrange an expedition. They arrive with a cargo of pots, bags, and other goods and depart with nuts and fishing nets.[4]

Social Structure

The primary division of the community is into two exogamous matrilineal moieties which are named after the hawk and the bat. The word for such a unit is *tina*, literally "mother," and the members are referred to collectively as "one blood" (*dara-ta*), though only when a genealogical connection can be traced or reasonably assumed do they consider themselves kin. The rare unions between men and women of the same group are held to be scandalous. It is believed that in the past the leaders would have demanded at least an immediate separation, perhaps would have had the offenders killed. Several examples are quoted in support of this belief, but whether these are historical or merely legendary is not clear. Nowadays the reaction is confined to adverse gossip. Sexual promiscuity before marriage is taken for granted, but the elders, if speaking in general terms, insist that casual relations within the moiety are wrong. They point out that if pregnancy follows and the woman has failed to admit the fault publicly, supernatural forces may cause difficulties during the child's birth (the guilty man is more fortunate—he escapes without punishment). The young folk, however, are disinclined to heed the warning—as are their seniors when planning adulterous intrigues—and in fact particular cases of moiety incest do not give rise to public criticism unless the couple have been blatant in their flouting of the conventions.

The manifestations of hostility so often encountered in a moiety organization are not features of the Wogeo system. Instead the reverse holds. True, a father is permitted to scold or whip his son, but contemporaries from opposite sides have to be circum-

[4]I. Hogbin, "Trading Expeditions in Northern New Guinea," *Oceania*, Vol. 5 (1934–1935), pp. 375–407.

spect with one another. The regulations are relaxed for a few minutes on certain ritual occasions; otherwise a man from the hawk group who insults or strikes someone from the bat group, or a man from the bat group who insults or strikes someone from the hawk group, can regain a good name only by handing over a pig or a basket of valuables in expiation of the offense.

Reciprocal obligations are also prescribed. Thus the men of one moiety are expected to initiate the boys of the other, and at funerals the gravediggers should belong to a different unit from that of the dead person. But, as we shall see, responsibilities of this kind are sometimes disregarded.

The inhabitants of a village form a local unit, but each unit is split into two, and usually the halves are more important than the whole. (One settlement has three sections but is treated as an anomaly and can be ignored.) Recruitment to this type of grouping is not defined by unilineal descent, and for an understanding of the principles it is necessary to know something about leadership, rights to land, and kinship.

The office of headman (*kokwal*) depends on familiarity with a corpus of mythology, with the magical spells therein set out, and with the performance of a variety of ritual procedures. An old leader may transmit such information only to the eldest son of one of his wives, but, as he is likely to have several, there is almost always a number of young men eligible for the choice. Should the heir selected be still a child, then an uncle, or even an aunt, can act as a trustee until such time as the boy is old enough to receive the inheritance. Thus, although succession is hereditary in the male line, it does not proceed automatically. The new title holder must be the firstborn of his mother but need not be his father's firstborn.[5]

Every village has a pair of headmen, each with a following of

---

[5] I. Hogbin, "The Father Chooses His Heir," *Oceania*, Vol. II (1940-1941), pp. 1-40. I have used the term "headman" in each of several publications dealing with Melanesian political organization, in Malaita, in Busama, in Guadalcanal, and Wogeo. Latterly it has become customary to speak of "big man" (see, for example, M. D. Sahlins, "Poor Man, Rich Man, Big Man, Chief," *Comparative Studies in Society and History*, Vol. 5, pp. 285-300). There is an argument for the new expression where leadership is achieved, but in Wogeo it is ascribed, and "headman" seems still to be preferable.

some of his close relatives. The majority of these relatives are his agnates, or believe themselves so to be, but often one or two trace their relationship through the mother or the father's mother. The headmen's dwellings are situated one at either end of the club, with, in theory and usually in practice, those of their respective sets of relatives in the immediate vicinity. The plan of the average settlement thus shows two clusters of houses with a meeting place in between. The notable exceptions are the villages in the Bukdi district, where the rugged topography is a complication. In Gol, for example, the club straddles a narrow ridge and the houses form two parallel rows in front.

Outsiders speak of the garden areas surrounding a village as the joint property of the inhabitants, making no reference to the rights of individuals to particular plots. But examination reveals first a line of demarcation cutting through the center, with each part associated with a headman and his coresident followers, and then further boundaries subdividing the sections into blocks of varying sizes, from one to several acres. Headman and follower alike have exclusive rights to a separate series of blocks—fifteen, twenty, sometimes more. Here the man and his family plant their taro, yams, and fruit and nut trees and collect the wild products. From time to time relatives may offer him the temporary use of a small area where they are making gardens, and from time to time he may invite them to come along with him, but always the bulk of his cultivations are concentrated on his own blocks.

Ordinarily land passes to the sons, with the eldest taking the largest share. The father indicates from their childhood which allotments each is to receive, and these they claim when about to marry. All must be given the portion due, and even a ne'er-do-well who has quarrelled with his parents or disgraced them cannot be disinherited. As might have been expected, most men prefer to live near the ground they cultivate. By this means they avoid lengthy journeys to work and save their wives from carrying the produce further than is necessary. It follows that the vast majority of the males remain for life in the village where they grew up. They build their houses alongside the father's, as he and his forebears also did in the past. Thus it is obvious why the male

Taro being prepared for a meal

residents of a housing cluster are mainly agnates.[6]

But men love all their children and wish to treat them alike. To do so is possible only for the wealthy, and even then none but a headman has enough blocks to give a reasonable number to more than one daughter. Such a father expects the girl in return to spend her life in his village. Accordingly, when she marries, instead of her joining the husband and the husband's agnates, the normal procedure, he is obliged to go over to hers. His brothers-

[6]I. Hogbin and P. Lawrence, *Studies in New Guinea Land Tenure.* (Sydney, 1967), pp. 1-44.

in-law arrange the construction of a dwelling, and it is here that the pair raise their family. She does not exercise the cultivation rights herself—women never do—but entrusts them to the man. On her death they pass to the sons, who also, of course, inherit in the usual way from their father. Generally they agree to make an equitable division. Those who take the mother's land remain in her housing cluster, whereas those who take the father's migrate at marriage to the place whence he came. The move does not cause an emotional wrench, for they seldom have to go far, never more than a few miles; moreover, from birth they will have had frequent contact with the new companions.

The presence of a few nonagnates in the cluster is now explained. These persons are derived from a female agnate of the men forming the core, a woman whose father was able to endow her with land.

Sometimes one or two other men are also included. A quarrel between brothers can lead to such ill feeling that some of them decide to link up with a relative elsewhere, or a man may be drawn by deep affection to construct a house alongside that of a kinsman of his wife. Migrants of this kind are still obliged, nevertheless, to make most of their gardens on their own blocks in the natal village. Eventually the inconvenience of traveling to and fro forces them to return.

The residents of a housing cluster are verbally distinguishable by reference to their headman, as, for instance, Marigum's or Bagasal's people in Dap or Kawang's or Janggara's people in Gol; but there is no single native term that can be applied to them. Further, in the popular view they do not form a group in the social sense at all. That they can be isolated on the ground, with dwellings in a separate corner of the village, is regarded as irrelevant, and I was repeatedly informed that they do not on that account have any special mutual claims or special reciprocal duties. What is supposed to be vital is not this small selection of relatives but the total of the cognates, all the men and all the women with whom a person has, or believes he has, genealogical ties. It is incumbent on him to help the lot of them, to stand by them, and to rally to their defense should the need arise. He must behave so that they will be prepared to place implicit trust in him, and, correspondingly, their conduct ought to be such that he will have complete faith in them. He and they are together against the world, ever generous to one another, upright, forgiving, fair, just, and honorable. The ideal is summed up by the word sometimes used. A man may speak of his cognates as his *warowaro*, from *waro*, a tough forest liana that grows into an impenetrable barrier (*waro* is also the word for the conical headdress, and it is tempting to see a connection, though this is denied). *Dan* is heard on occasion, but the older villagers say that the usage is incorrect and that the word ought to be restricted to agnates. The expression will not do for the residential cluster, which excludes some agnates and includes some nonagnates. The literal meaning of *dan* is "water," here a euphemism for semen. Why a people not normally squeamish in discussing sexual matters openly should suddenly prefer a genteelism remains unexplained.

When speaking in this context of the cognates, the natives seldom mention the affines, who in practice turn out to be almost, if not quite, as important. A person has weighty obligations to both the close relatives of his spouse and the spouses of his close relatives. He is expected to be as ready to help his brother-in-law as his brother and, for that matter, to take part in the expedition to carry out revenge if either the one or the other should be murdered.

Groupings of cognates—kindreds, as we may call them—are not eternal like a unilineal moiety, where the newly born members continually replace those who die. Every individual is the focal point of a unique kindred, which exists only so long as he remains alive. A society organized on a basis of unilineal groups can be represented diagramatically by a figure neatly divided into segments; a society of kindreds is more like a series of overlapping circles.

By comparison with many of the Pacific islanders, the Wogeo are not good genealogists. A few can give the name of a great-great-grandfather, but ordinarily the limit is reached by an enumeration of four or five of the great-grandparents with a list of their descendants. Thus, although the majority of the householders of a cluster think of themselves as agnates, as has been mentioned, often the clusters are made up of two or more branches and the members are unaware of how precisely these are united. Should there be, say, ten adult males, then each of two lots of five may be able to give the full details of their relationships without anyone knowing who was the ancestor common to them all or how long ago he was alive. If this state of affairs obtains with those from next door, we need not be surprised at the vagueness of the information available about the connections with some of the persons from beyond the village borders. Yet everyone counts his kinsmen by the hundred. He is convinced that somehow he is bound to the entire population of his district and to a large number of people from other districts, always more than half the inhabitants of the island. A supposed tie between two seniors is sufficient justification for their respective offspring to say that therefore they too must be kin. The absence of any bias in favor of moiety members is to be noted.

Probably the shallowness of the genealogies also accounts for the fact that the link for the nonagnates in a cluster is either the man's mother or his father's mother, never a female ancestor from further back. Once the names of the great-grandmothers and great-great-grandmothers are forgotten, a spurious claim to agnatic relationship is unlikely to be challenged, especially when no advantage is sought.

The kinship nomenclature is of classificatory type, modeled on the pattern known as Iroquois. The sibling terms are applied to the parallel cousins, but there is a special term for the cross cousins; the father term is applied to the father's brothers and the mother term to the mother's sisters and the father's sisters, but there is a special term for the mother's brothers; and the son and daughter terms are applied to brothers' children and to sisters' children (woman speaking), but there is a special term for sisters' children (man speaking).[7] These terms can be legitimately extended to all cognates, irrespective of whether the bonds are known or assumed. The scores in the first ascending generation are fathers, mothers, or mother's brothers; those in the same generation brothers, sisters, or cross cousins; those in the first descending generation sons, daughters, or sisters' children.

[7] I. Hogbin, "Wogeo Kinship Terminology," *Oceania*, Vol. 34 (1963-1934), pp. 308-309.

The affines are fitted neatly into the scheme. There is a special term for the son- and daughter-in-law, the parents-in-law, and the brothers and sisters of the parents-in-law; and another special term for the wife's brother, the husband's sister, the sister's husband (man speaking), and the brother's wife (woman speaking). But all the rest are referred to by terms applied to the cognates. Therefore, an aunt's husband is the same as a father, and an uncle's wife is the same as a mother. A man also speaks of his sisters-in-law as though they were mothers.

To insist that everyone ought to collaborate constantly with such a vast assembly is unrealistic. In building his house, a man may perhaps be grateful for the help of sixty, seventy, even eighty adults, but for no task does he need hundreds. Probably most of his jobs, indeed, are best carried out by less than a dozen working together. He may be pleased to have cognates and affines in a village eight miles away, the maximum distance possible, when trouble arises or on other odd occasions, as, for example, if his life is threatened or he is short of a pig for some village ceremony; but certainly he would never dream of going to them for an hour's loan of an axe or for half-a-day's assistance in clearing land for an ordinary garden. Why should he, when it is easier to approach someone nearer home?

If pressed, people are ready to admit that their descriptions of the ideal situation are exaggerated. They agree that they like to concentrate on what ought to happen at the expense of what actually takes place. "Yes, you're right. We approach our close relatives often, our distant relatives seldom," they told me. "But our distant relatives are still there waiting." Genealogical propinquity is here implied, but, unlike some New Guinea societies, the Wogeo do not have a strict definition of what constitutes a close kinsman.[8] So, while one person may point to a second cousin to whom he is devoted, another may attempt to deny the status to a first cousin he happens to dislike. We have thus

[8]A Busama, for example, defines his close relatives as his grandparents, their children and grandchildren, his parents' grandchildren, and his own grand-children. These are "one blood" (*da-tigeng*) as distinct from the rest of his cognates, who are "one stem" (*bu-tigeng*). See I. Hogbin, *Kinship and Marriage in a New Guinea Village* (London 1963), p. 14.

to accept a blurred zone of discrimination instead of a sharp line.

This concession does not go far enough. It ignores geographical propinquity, inasmuch as the relatives in a housing cluster are next-door neighbors. They can scarcely avoid spending hours in one another's company. They walk along the same paths to the gardens, which are often adjoining or if not then within hailing distance; they fish off the same reefs and beach their canoes on the same stretch of shore line; and they sit in the evenings in the same club. They may not have special mutual claims and duties, as is so stoutly maintained, but inevitably they make a habit of activating the potentials of their relationships and carry out much of their work together. I do not mean that they are always, or even usually, by themselves; the point is that they make up a regular nucleus for all types of cooperation. One day a few outside uncles, cousins, or affines may join in with them, another day a different series joins; but throughout, the core remains relatively unchanged, allowing that on a particular occasion somebody may be absent, returning the help previously given to him by an uncle, cousin, or affine. It is significant also that the headman's authority is exercised primarily over his fellows within the cluster and that when he makes a contribution to a feast he does so in their names as well as his own.

Certainly it would be a grave mistake to underestimate the importance of the wide circle of cognates, but in the light of the foregoing discussion I have no hesitation in contradicting the statement that the households of the cluster do not form a social group. The truth is that they belong to a distinct and perpetual corporate entity, occupying their own territory, pooling labor, and owing allegiance to an hereditary leader. Unfortunately neither of the common terms, clan and lineage, is applicable. The criterion for membership is filiation—being the child of a particular parent, usually the father, occasionally the mother—and hence inheriting that parent's land rights. Cumulative filiation over the generations leads to the husbands in a cluster becoming a putative cognatic descent group, but as this condition is a by-product and not an essential, probably the expression should also be avoided. Thus there appears to be no alternative to the retention of my original phrase, the residents of the housing cluster, awkward and clumsy though it is.[9]

It remains to speak briefly of the marriage regulations. These are simple. I have pointed out that the moieties are exogamous. In addition, unions are prohibited between close kin, interpreted in this context as those who regularly work side by side. "If a boy is accustomed to taking food from a girl's hand, then she is like a sister and cannot be his wife," it is explained. This means that he may not look for a bride among the daughters of the men of his housing cluster and usually not among his first cousins from outside. Whether some of his second cousins from outside are forbidden depends on his parents' and his own previous relations with them. There is no such thing as a total ban on the girls from the housing cluster at the other end of the village, and should the formal requirements be satisfied a match can go ahead.

Parents arrange the marriage of firstborn sons and firstborn daughters, but allow the younger members of the family to choose for themselves. The ideal mate for an eldest son is his father's father's eldest sister's eldest son's eldest daughter, but more often than not the disparity in age is too great.[10]

Adultery is common and is ordinarily disapproved, though there may be extenuating circumstances, provided one of the couple is not married to a close relative of the other.[11] If one of them is, they both risk death through the intervention of supernatural forces.

[9]In earlier publications, although the facts were recorded, I have wavered between clan, lineage, and descent group. It should also be pointed out that some anthropologists would not approve the term cognatic descent group. These writers insist that descent groups must be either strictly patrilineal or strictly matrilineal.

[10]I. Hogbin and P. Lawrence, *Studies in New Guinea Land Tenure* (Sydney 1967), pp. 24-25.

[11]I. Hogbin, "Social Reaction to Crime: Law and Morals in the Schouten Islands," *Journal of the Royal Anthropological Institute*, Vol. 68 (1938), pp. 223-262.

II   Culture Heroes

I shall begin my study of Wogeo religion with an account of
the beliefs about spirits. Such beings are divided into various
classes, each designated by a special term. Those to be considered
in the present chapter are known as the *nanarang*, a word best
translated as "culture heroes."[1] Other classes are discussed in the
next chapter.

The culture heroes created order out of primeval chaos; they
molded the physical environment, discovered the usefulness of
trees and plants, invented tools and weapons, originated local
customs, and, directly or indirectly, devised the systems of magic.
Each one looked and acted like a human being—male or female;
old or young; loving or hating; being born, marrying, raising a
family, or dying—but they were not in fact flesh and blood. Eventually the majority of them vanished, and at once mortal men
appeared, real people like ourselves. Nobody speculates about
whence these original ancestors came or even how, if the teachers
had already disappeared, they could have acquired the proper
techniques and deduced the established standards. The villagers
of today say simply that the heroes on departing took only the
shadow (*vanunu*) of things, leaving behind for you and me the
objects themselves (*ramata*, literally "persons").

The local notion is that the earth is like a huge platter with
raised edges and the sky above a shallow upturned bowl. At the

---

[1]Similar spirit categories are common in western Melanesia, and pidgin English, the lingua franca of modern New Guinea, has developed a series of expressions of general application. Culture heroes are referred to as *masalai*, a term
probably derived from the language of Blanche Bay in eastern New Britain, site
of an early trading post. Some writers translate *masalai* as "deities," but in my view
this translation is misleading.

27

center of the platter, beneath the highest point of the bowl, is
Wogeo itself, the one place that has been there always, home of
the heroes and of mankind. Radiating outwards, in the positions
allocated by the same heroes, are the other islands and the moon
and the stars. A natural corollary is the assumption that Wogeo
practice is alone valid and Wogeo speech uniquely pure. Therefore, the people refuse to speak the languages of the communities
with which they trade. "If these folk are so stupid as to ignore the
model set by the culture heroes and instead imitate the barking
of dogs, that's their business; but you'll agree we're right in despis-
ing them," a friend remarked. (The few foreigners I was able to
question had other views. They treated such judgments as laugha-
ble, denied knowledge of the names and doings of the Wogeo
culture heroes, and preferred rather to exalt their own. Social
intercourse between the different groups is maintained by each
learning to understand—"to hear" is the native phrase—the
speech of the rest.)

In everyday life the heroes are most significant as the final
authority for conduct. The invariable answer to questions about
the reason for a particular custom is that the heroes so decreed.
In some parts of Melanesia (for instance, Malaita) the response in
similar contexts is, "That's the proper thing to do; we've always
done it in that way." Both types of reply indicate a reverence for
precedent, but the Wogeo appeal to the supernatural means that
here irregularity is treated not only as immoral but also as sinful.
Whether as a consequence innovations are less acceptable I cannot
say, but my guess is that secular scruples are no easier to overcome
than religious scruples.

The Mythology

Discussion of the heroes demands consideration of the narratives setting out their exploits. The accounts are spoken of as
nanasa to distinguish them from two other types of stories, the
sigilagila and the *filava*. The *sigilagila* are described as fictional.
Nearly all the main characters are animals or birds with the power
of speech, and, as in Aesop's fables, there is usually an obvious
moral. Everyone remembers a collection of such folk tales, which

he relates for entertainment or, in a more serious vein, to suggest
to the children that naughtiness—disobedience, rudeness, stealing, telling lies, or whatever it is—leads to unpleasant consequences. The word *filava*, by contrast, applies primarily to
legends—though it is derived from *fila*, "to speak," and therefore
covers news, gossip, and, indeed, any statement about actual persons, living or dead. Such reports the listener is free to accept or
reject according to circumstances, including those of prior knowledge. But the *nanasa* are religious myths. The people maintain
that all are sacred, and when discussing the subject in a general
way they reiterate that the whole population accepts them as
absolutely true. We shall see presently that this is not strictly
accurate, for although the bulk of the mythology gives rise to
neither doubt nor criticism, quarrels may occur over certain parts
of it when each side quotes a private version in substantiation of
a particular claim.

It should be noted also that *nanasa* are not surrounded by an
air of great solemnity. A narrator who happens to have a sense of
theater may turn them into dramatic performances, altering his
voice to indicate the different individuals concerned, and if the
incidents are amusing the members of his audience laugh openly,
passing jesting—even lewd—comments. I admit that several people remarked that a man or woman who presumes to expound a
myth before sunset runs the risk of being stricken with boils, but
I never knew of anyone taking the warning seriously, or, for that
matter, attributing subsequent illness or misadventure to a breach
of the taboo.

The era of the myths is outside recorded time, which only
begins with the ancestors. A hero's doings are never dated,
whereas frequently a legendary event is given historical authen-
ticity by a statement of its having taken place at a definite period.
The stock phrase is, "My grandfather's father was not alive then,
but he told my grandfather, who told my father, who in turn told
me, that he had seen an old coconut palm that was planted while
all this was going on." (The life of a coconut palm is about 70 or
80 years, an interval taken to cover three generations.)

An analysis of the myths, far from building up a coherent body
of doctrine, reveals the same sort of haphazard world as that of the

Just-So stories. There are contradiction, duplications, repetitions, and even some notable omissions. Thus neither the moiety division nor the introduction of fire is accounted for. When gaps of this kind are pointed out the people shrug their shoulders and answer that, nevertheless, positively everything did come from the heroes.

Geographical and Technological Myths

The least complicated of the myths, notable also for their lack of an accompanying system of magic, are those of the extensive series accounting for foreign places. Universally known, they are expounded without further restrictions than those imposed by the ordinary rules of etiquette (as, for example, that young people, boys as well as girls, should not hold forth, unless deliberately encouraged, in the presence of their elders). There is in each case a standard rendition, and if a speaker omits incidents, or tells them in the wrong order, those present, while carefully—even ostentatiously—avoiding interruption, indicate disapprobation by a raised eyebrow, a shake of the head, or a sniff.

No area with which the people are familiar is forgotten, though sometimes a foreigner may find identification difficult. The Wogeo names do not always coincide with those used on the spot or with those employed by Europeans, and often there are separate terms for the districts of an island but none for the island as a whole. Usually the story has a concealed moral in that the principal character was changed into the geographical feature after committing an act that is socially reprehensible—perhaps he was brutal or unkind, or he may have stolen or seduced the wife of a neighbor. But it is a safe generalization that the moral of a myth is never underlined, as always happens with folk tales.

The myths of Tidalap and Dunga-Kwab-Dap are typical. Like all the earliest culture heroes, Tidalap belonged to Wogeo. On reaching manhood he took a hero girl from a village nearby as his wife. In the beginning everything went well, but he was by nature suspicious and soon accused her of infidelity. Although she protested innocence, he not only refused to listen but beat her so unmercifully that the blood flowed from the wounds. His relatives, fearing her kinsmen might take vengeance on them for failing to prevent such cruelty, decided to launch their canoes and sail away. Tidlap, now alone, became terrified also and followed. But his brothers, in the interests of their own safety, killed him and dismembered the body. The trunk turned into the island of Mushu, which is low and flat, the head into the hilly island of Kairiru, the fingers into various coral reefs, and the legs into the Torricelli Mountains of the New Guinea mainland.

Dunga-Kwab-Dap suspected two heroes from his settlement of stealing his coconuts, and in anger he scattered food remains on their bedding to bring the ants during the night to irritate them. They hurled a flaming log at him, and one half of his body became the island of Manam and the other half Bam, two active volcanoes visible from the mountain above Dap village on the east side of Wogeo (Dunga-Kwab-Dap means literally "within the forest of Dap village").

The myths of the heavenly bodies are equally straightforward and devoid of magical associations. I have selected that relating to the moon.

Originally the culture heroes could work continuously, in the earlier hours by the light of the sun and later in the day by that of the full moon, which regularly rose at dusk. But a famine occurred, and one of the heroes, desperately in need of food for his family, shot the moon down with his spear. It proved to be like a great bird, so he trussed it in a basket, which he hung in a corner of the house. Then, warning his daughter and young son to eat sparingly, he set out to fish. The pair took little pieces at a time, but despite their precautions the last remaining fragment slipped through the meshes of the basket, turned into the complete bird again, and flew back to the sky. From that moment, in revenge, the moon has waxed and waned, giving illumination for only a part of the time. The two children, fearful of their father's rage, fled to the forest, where the bush hero Ngabilkala married the girl. He treated her well but was so jealous of the brother that the lad chose the consequences of returning home. There he related what had happened. The bushman set out in pursuit, but the hero-villagers came to the rescue and slew him with carefully aimed oven stones. Each one as it fell to the ground caused a hot spring to gush forth, and these can be seen to this day. The body was smashed and pulverized, with the penis the only recognizable part remaining. This the sorrowing widow took and buried under the forest dwelling. In the ground the organ turned into a giant taro (*ngabira*), a source of extra food when feasts are held.

No explanation is forthcoming for interest in the moon and in a vegetable being expressed in the same myth. A possible reason could be that this kind of taro, which is phallic in shape, grows only in the forest, and it is in the forest that young couples meet on moonlit nights for secret lovemaking.

The other food crops also have a link with the sky. The relevant myth—again common knowledge and lacking in magic—is remarkable in that not one of the heroes concerned is given a name. Less striking, because so characteristic, are the inherent inconsistencies—the incidental reference to somebody's being offered taro before he achieves its discovery and to somebody else's receiving taro skins when, on the evidence provided, taro could not have been available.

An aged hero suffering from a malarial ague retired to the clubhouse and there requested some youths, who were chatting in a corner, to kindle a small fire under his bed to keep him warm. While doing so they noticed his testes hanging through the interstices of the canes, and as a joke they took an ant to bite him. Furious, he recited a spell (which the ancestors omitted to obtain) to make the offenders shrink in size. Then he drove them into the slit of a wooden gong, which he cast into the sea. Eventually the gong floated to the New Guinea mainland, where one of the local heroes (whose forefathers must, of course, have come from Wogeo), mistaking it for driftwood, smashed it with his axe. Out sprang the boys, all ravenously hungry after their long confinement. The hero invited them to his village for a meal, but they feared he might be a cannibal. One only was prepared to take the risk, and the rest pretended to have a sore leg, a swollen foot, a cut toe, or some other disability. Their suspicions proved to be justified, and when the hero returned with food they saw the finger of their companion in the middle of the dish. This was all that remained of the body.

The lads now dispersed, and the fate of the youngest is alone recorded. He hid in the branches of a tree, but the hero soon discovered him and determined to have him for the cooking pot. "How did you get up there?" he asked. "I came up feet first," the boy replied. The hero tried to ascend upside down and succeeded only in making his nose bleed. Meantime lice from the boy's head had crawled on to the tree, where they changed into termites. It is fitting that such destructive insects should have appeared first in an outlandish area. Not till later did they spread to inflict Wogeo.

After an interval a hawk saw the boy high up in the tree and took pity on him. It picked him up in its beak and carried him off to the sky above his Wogeo home. He looked down and, seeing his mother beneath, threw her a coconut. The nut was green when it left his hands, but, so great was the distance of its fall, that the husk was already brown and shrivelled when it reached her feet. Ignorant of the uses of a coconut, she left it lying on the ground. In due course it began to sprout and eventually grew to be a palm so tall that the leaves brushed against the underside of the sky.

By now the boy's father decided that his son must have perished. He organized a great funeral feast and invited all the villagers to attend. But he was careless in distributing the food, and when the turn of two young orphans came nothing remained but pork bones, areca-nut husks, and taro skins. The pair were so disgusted that they determined to go away. They climbed the giant coconut palm, mounting upwards day after day, until by the time they had reached the top they were fully grown men. The boy, now adult also, made them welcome, and all three loaded baskets with ornaments, areca nuts, bananas, and taro and descended to earth. The people, who had never seen any of these things before, conferred the title of headman upon them as a mark of honor.

The myths telling of the invention of such technical items as fishhooks, stone adzes, and baskets are in most respects similar. The following tale relates to fishhooks.

At first the culture heroes went fishing on the reef with their bare hands—and, naturally, were seldom successful. But the hero Kafato had the notion of shaping a hook from a piece of shell and attaching it to a line and rod. This solved the problem, and each day he made a fine catch. He was by nature selfish, nevertheless, and always kept the fish for himself. Another hero, anxious to learn the secret, hid behind a pile of rocks. As soon as Kafato approached, this person jumped out and hit him on the head with a stick. The thief then took the hook away, leaving his victim lying like a corpse. After an interval someone who was sympathetic aroused poor Kafato by inserting a stalk of spidery grass in his nostrils to bring on a bout of sneezing (as is still done to anyone who has fainted). He quickly pulled himself together and was soon devising other kinds of hooks.

Myths and Institutions

The next series of myths is concerned with such fundamentals as the sexual division of labour, marriage and the mutual responsibilities of husband and wife, revenge, and leadership. As with the stories already considered, these are familiar to the majority of the islanders. The details of the magic enshrined in them, however, are the sole property of specialists, whose duty it is to perform the rites for the benefit of others, sometimes a section of the village, sometimes its entire population. As an example, there is the myth incorporating the magic to endow the members of a trading expedition with such good looks that their exchange partners will be overcome with awe and offer rich gifts. The tale is repeated in the same form throughout the two districts that take part in the voyages, but in every settlement the magic belongs to but a single individual, who has inherited the secrets from his predecessors. As might have been expected, the sets of spells are nearly identical, with but slight variations of phrasing.

Occasionally two separate myths give the origin of a single institution. In such a case, although a householder may be acquainted with both, and his village include a pair of magicians capable of carrying out the rites independently, he tends to exercise a preference, the result either of a closer kinship tie with one of the specialists or a greater confidence in the man's powers.

I shall quote the companion myths relating to marriage. The first tells of the culture heroine Jari, who, with that lack of logic that is so common, inaugurated the wedded state not with her initial match but with her second. She was the daughter of a snake woman, a fact she concealed from her husband. It was her practice to wait till he had gone out fishing before summoning her mother to the house to care for their infant while she herself worked in the gardens. One afternoon he returned early and, alarmed at the sight of the baby encircled by the serpent's coils, killed the reptile with his axe. Jari was heartbroken at the loss of her parent and declined to stay. She took the precaution of piling the house, the cooking pots, and a basket of taro into her vulva and then went over to the other side of the island. There, while walking along the shore, she saw a man fishing from the branch of a *Callophyllum* tree that overhung the water. This was Kamarong, a wild culture hero from the forest. "Tell me where your dwelling is that I may take shelter," she called to him. But he only shook his head, for he had no conception of what the word "dwelling" meant. Accordingly, Jari took poles, rafters, walls, and thatch from her vulva and put up a residence for them both. "Now, where are the cooking pots?" she asked. Again he shook his head—his food had hitherto consisted solely of fish smoked over the fire. "Well, if I supply the pots, will you show me your gardens?" Jari now enquired. As he was also ignorant of agriculture she was forced to delve once more and produce her own taro. Kamarong was delighted with the meal and agreed to clear an area of ground for her. "I'll bring home fish if you will become my wife and do the cultivation and cooking," he said. She hesitated to accept the proposal because he stank so abominably. The poor fellow had no anus and was obliged to use his mouth for evacuating as well as for swallowing. After some thought she made him bend over with his head towards the ground. She then took a length of bamboo and pierced his rectum. At last she could live with him. These two, Jari and Kamarong, were the first married couple. She worked in the gardens and cooked the food, and he spent his days fishing, activities in which their respective magic remains effective.

The leading characters of the second story are the two brothers Tamwatara-Bitang and Tamwatara-Sik (that is, Big and Little Tamwatara) and the two sisters Jina and Kasuara. One day when the girls' mother's fire had gone out she sent them to ask the

youths for a live ember so that she might rekindle it. The pair
argued over which of them should make the request, and Jina, as
the elder, carried the day. Before returning home she remarked
casually that the taro was ready for cooking. The brothers had
never tasted cultivated vegetables and decided that one of them
ought to invite this girl to share the house and prepare the meals,
thereby establishing the custom of marriage. Again there was a
quarrel over the privilege, and once more it was the elder, Tamwatara-Bitang, who won. The girls disputed the proposal also, but
Jina shamed Kasuara into silence by insisting that the firstborn
must always be wed before the juniors in the family. Then she
oiled and painted her body, took a new set of skirts, adorned
herself with ornaments, and went off in the wake of her suitor. On
the way, while she paused to rest by a stream, the toothless old
hag Vina approached and pretended to point out a pretty bird
perched in a tree. As Jina turned her face upwards to look the
woman threw a handful of lime and blinded her. Vina now seized
all the bridal finery and donned them. In due course she presented
herself at the house of Tamwatara-Bitang, who accepted her as his
wife.

Next day Tamwatara-Sik took his spears to hunt wild pig. Soon
he came across the injured Jina crawling along the banks of a
stream. He rubbed saliva into her eyes, and immediately her sight
was restored. (This incident provided the magic for the prows of
new canoes to make certain that they will aim straight for their
destination and not drift with the current.) Then he brought her
a garment to cover her nakedness and led her to the village, where
she made gardens for him and cooked his food. Tamwatara-Bitang
came to realize that he had been tricked, but he thought it best to
hold his tongue.

Eventually Jina became pregnant and bore Tamwatara-Sik a
son, whom they called Lelenga. Vina fooled Tamwatara-Bitang
for a short while by blowing her belly up with wind but in the end
was forced to admit to him that she was long past the menopause.
Filled with envy of his more fortunate younger brother, he took
a club and slew him. The origin of killing is thus to be sought in
fratricide. When Lelenga grew up he avenged the murder by
stabbing his uncle through the heart. Soon he developed into such

a redoubtable warrior that his enemies took counsel together that they might be rid of him. He sensed their jealousy and made up his mind to escape with his mother to the mainland. Accordingly, he carved a wooden likeness of himself and fixed it in the floor of his house near the doorway. As he hoped, the vain attempts to execute this dummy delayed the attacking party, and the pair was able to push off from the shore unseen.

The emphasis in both these myths on the economic rather than the sexual side of the marriage relationship calls for some comment. In communities where a high value is set on premarital chastity the desire for sexual gratification is likely to be an important motive for entering into an alliance, but since in Wogeo youths and girls are promiscuous, the question does not arise.

The friction over the precedence due to older brothers and older sisters will also have been noted. This friction is a commonplace of Wogeo life and often crops up in the myths, as do various other everyday actions. The people do not go out of their way to stress the heroes' ultimate responsibility, but a person upset by a brother's insults, a distant kinsman's lack of charity, or some other misconduct is apt to comfort himself with such a remark as, "What else is to be expected? Didn't such-and-such a hero behave just like that?" Thus the myth accounting for polygyny and the resulting domestic discord is heard most frequently from the husbands of compound households where the wives cause embarrassment by continual bickering.

The first culture hero to have two spouses was Takume. One of them, Wutmara, was a culture heroine, but Takume had also married a ghost in the afterworld. Wutmara suggested that to save himself the exhaustion of the long journeys to see this being he should bring it to share the dwelling in Wogeo. He agreed, not realizing that she had determined on murder. She pretended good fellowship with the ghost and next morning asked its help to collect firewood. But at the first opportunity she hit it on the head with a heavy pole and left it for dead in the forest. Either she forgot or did not know that ghosts are immortal. It quickly recovered from the blow, hid among the undergrowth till nightfall, and then went back to the village to avenge itself by transposing the genital organs of Takume and Wutmara. The pair were greatly inconvenienced—neither knew what to do when urinating, and their movements in sexual intercourse were grotesque (the narration of this episode, if ably mimed, can reduce a gathering to helpless laughter). After a time the ghost listened to their entreaties and changed them back again, though so bitter was it with Wutmara that it sewed up her vagina, and she soon died in agony of a burst bladder. Then it shrank in size and fastened itself on Takume's pubic hairs so that he would have to carry it about. He grew weary of the burden and worked out a scheme to be free. He persuaded it to let go while he climbed a tree to gather fruit for a snack. "Stand clear," he shouted. "Stay where I can see you. I don't want to drop anything on your head." But as soon as it moved into the open he began pelting it with stones that he had ready in his basket. It collapsed, and he abandoned the apparently lifeless body just as Wutmara had done earlier. Many months afterwards, while he was out hunting, he found a new kind of palm. This was the original coconut. He took one of the nuts and, to test whether it was poisonous, fed it to his dogs. They ate the flesh with relish and suffered no ill effects. Next he tried a piece on his mother. She grated the flesh and squeezed out the liquid, thereby discovering coconut cream, the great culinary delicacy. Then she heated the cream until it clarified and became coconut oil, the main Wogeo aid to beauty. Takume decided that now he could taste with safety, but when he picked up the nut he saw marks at one end. In these he recognized the face of his ghost wife reproaching him.

Topographical Myths

Although Wogeo, taken as a whole, did not have to be created, culture heroes are still said to have shaped some of the minor topographical details. The relevant myths are of two types. In one, scenic items considered by the people themselves to be unpleasant or incommoding seem to be the prime concern; in the other, landscape appears only as an afterthought. I shall begin with the former group. The stories are recounted and discussed all round the island, but each is in some degree the property of the inhabitants of the district or settlement where the features in question are to be found; moreover, these persons—or, rather, certain specialists among them—have proprietary rights in the magic. Accordingly, if one such individual happens to be present in a gathering when the subject comes up in conversation, the rest leave the commentary to him. I shall open with an example from Bukdi district.

Gale, a culture hero of Dap, on returning from a visit to Bukdi, complained that his hosts had not given him enough to eat. "They think only of entertaining headmen; other folk are nothing to them and find themselves shamefully neglected," he reported. The Bukdi, pained by the criticism, begged him to come again. He accepted the invitation, and now they furnished lavish hospitality. His greed knew no limits, and his belly grew more and more distended. In the end, when he could no longer move his jaws for weariness, he asked if they would allow him to take the remaining bananas home to eat later. They loaded him till he could barely stagger under the burden, and the road he took from Gol village has ever since had such a steep gradient that a person descending runs the risk of falling headlong. A short distance further on he suffered from an attack of diarrhea, which resulted in the path becoming almost impassable in wet weather on account of the heavy clay. Then suddenly the gases escaping from his belly made him belch until he blew himself up. Today his bones are visible as a barren outcrop of white limestone. This myth has furnished the Bukdi leaders with magic that expands the food supplies on the occasion of feasts till the guests are sickened by the quantity.

My second tale comes from the Bagiau district. A bush hero overheard two village heroines arranging an expedition to seek shellfish that evening. Later he approached one of them, sent her away on an errand, and then proceeded to impersonate her. He now suggested to the other that she leave her baby with him and take the first turn on the reef. Unaware of the fraud, she departed; and at once he began devouring the child. The mother heard its cries and hurried back to suckle it. All became clear from a glance at its hand, which was chewed to the bone. She handed the baby back, ran over the reef, and stuck her torch in a cleft in the rocks to make the hero think she was still there. She assured herself that it would go on burning for some time and then fled. But so terrified was she that a trail of feces marked her progress. This trail became an extensive swamp that has remained an inconvenience to travelers, who are forced to deviate for a mile or more around the edge. The torch also is visible as an isolated pinnacle above the reach of the highest tides. This myth provides the Bagiau residents with magic to prolong the glow of their fishing flares.

The third illustration, from the Wonevaro area, is concerned with both topography and village specialities. The hero was Tawawa, who fooled the inhabitants of the different settlements one after the other. His escapades opened in Mwarok, in the southwest, near the Bagiau boundary. Here he persuaded several children to mount their swing simultaneously. He climbed the tree from which it was suspended, cut the rope half way through, and then made off surreptitiously for Kinaba. Within a few minutes the swing came crashing down. The rope flew into the air with great force, and today a ravine marks the spot where it fell to the ground. The children were all killed and changed into stones. As a consequence, the Mwarok agricultural lands are full of coral boulders and are notoriously infertile. Only with the performance of Tawara's magic is the disadvantage overcome and good harvests can be obtained.

In Kinaba Tawawa insisted that rat meat was equal in flavor to pork and persuaded the householders to try it. When satisfied that every oven was full of rat carcasses, he went on to Dap. The Kinaba ate heartily and became violently ill. The present-day residents of the village use Tawawa's magic and explained that this is why they own so many pigs; other people, however, point to the rats with which the place is said to be infested.

Tawawa had timed his Dap visit to coincide with a feast of Tahitian chestnuts. If the villagers cared to pick further supplies, he told them, he would husk those already gathered. Once the householders had departed he removed the bulk of the nuts and replaced them with pebbles, covering them over with a thin dressing of the nuts that remained. Then he moved on to Job. The Dap folk did not discover the hoax till they had their cooking pots ready. Cursing Tawawa roundly, they emptied the stones on Tabele Point nearby, where to this day the beach is strewn with

shingle. But the Dap chestnut trees, when strengthened by Tawawa's magic, are supposed to yield a bigger crop than those grow
ing elsewhere.

The Job folk were cutting sugar canes and tying them in bundles. Tawawa advised them to stand with the stalks upright and
to pass the rope behind their backs. Thus they fastened themselves, and the harder they pulled the more immobile they became. He sneaked off laughingly to Bariat, leaving rescue to a
casual passerby. Nowadays Job, thanks to Tawawa's magic, is
famous for its sugar.

In Bariat the breadfruit harvest was in full swing, and the men
were all up in the trees. As is usual to this day, they plucked the
fruit and lowered each one to the ground on a rope to prevent its
being bruised. Tawawa told them a better plan would be to fasten
one end of the rope around their neck and then let the other go.
But when they carried out his instructions they were pulled down
and ended up with broken legs. The Bariat trees, once bespelled
with Tawawa's magic, of course, have an outstanding yield.

Tawawa, having visited every Wonevaro village, now jour-
neyed northwards. He came upon a dwelling, and, hearing voices,
listened outside. The occupants, two housewives, were deciding
to gather chestnuts the following day. He went ahead to the
orchard and changed himself into a baby; the women found him
and carried him tenderly home. Here they fed him, but next
morning, after their departure for the gardens, he defecated in the
cooking pots. Again they gave him a meal, slept, and went off to
the cultivations; and again he fouled the pots. Soon they agreed
on what to do. When the sun rose, although both took baskets and
walked down the pathway into the bush, only one went on to the
garden plots. Here she began banging two sticks together to give
the impression that there was a couple of workers. Meantime the
other had doubled back to spy on Tawawa through a peephole in
the house wall. In the evening she was able to report that, indeed,
he was the culprit. He had become a man once more, defecated
in the pots, and changed back into a baby. The woman now filled
a large vessel with water, lighted a fire, and heated the contents
to boiling point. Then they seized Tawawa, popped him in,
quickly replaced the lid, and rolled the saucepan into the sea. As

it sank they saw a South Seas apple floating on the surface, and in the struggle to reach it both of them were drowned. For this reason the region beyond Bariat remains unpopulated, though people still go there to collect the wild South Seas apples.

The topographical myths of the second type deal primarily with the rights and privileges claimed by particular villages, and the account of the sudden appearance of a rock, spring, or whatever it may be—invariably something of no great significance— is added as a sort of epilogue, seemingly for the express purpose of establishing a tangible link between the heroic past and the present. The native attitude may be compared with that of the members of a European nation to a column erected to commemorate an earlier victory against an invading army or to a plaque let into the wall to indicate the spot where long ago some notable political martyr or reformer met his death. Such reminders bring history to life and give seeming proof that what is commonly held to have taken place did in fact happen.

As a rule, well-informed seniors from all over the island can give a bald outline of most of the narratives, but for a reasonably full version it is necessary to ask a person from the community immediately concerned, and if the finer points are required then there is but one recognized authority, a headman of the place, the person who in part owes his position to this special knowledge. As often as the occasion demands, he has the job of exactly repeating the recorded actions of the culture heroes. To this end he must be familiar, down to the minutest detail, with the successive procedures and allied rituals.

I shall open with the story of Mafofo, a culture hero from Dap revered by the villagers for his inaugurating trading voyages to the mainland. My first paragraph will indicate the elaborateness of the complete story, but the bare bones will suffice for our present purpose, and from then on I shall keep to the essentials.

Mafofo was the original Dap culture hero; he founded the settlement, and other heroes joined him later. The house that he and his wives occupied stood in the center of the village. He owned many Canarium-almond trees, and the women became expert in weaving fishing nets and small baskets. The idea came to him of offering some of the nuts, nets, and baskets to the culture heroes who had earlier left Wogeo for other places, including New Guinea itself, so that he might receive in exchange the things they possessed and he lacked, such as clay pots, big carrying bags, bamboo flutes, bird-of-paradise plumes and other feathers, and shell rings and cowries. So he decided to arrange with the Dap heroes for the fashioning of a great canoe, big enough for a crew and more than a dozen passengers and their cargo, and to invite the heroes from some of the other places to follow the example. He went into the forest and chose a tree of a certain species for the dugout. This the heroes from the village felled. To make sure that the finished canoe would be buoyant and sail against as well as with the wind, they observed various taboos. Thus they avoided their wives for a whole day before starting the job, and while actually at work they neither chewed betelnut nor smoked. Later, when engaged on the further construction, they took similar precautions. They trimmed the branches off, hollowed out some of the middle to reduce the weight of the log, and then hauled it down to the shore. Mafofo strode ahead along the path. He had made up his mind to call the canoe *Urem Tariga* (*tariga*, "reef heron"), and as he went along he chanted this magical spell to make it swift:

"*Urem Tariga,* your feet hasten, your blood hastens,
    Reef heron, reef heron.
Your vitals hasten, your liver hastens, your bowels hasten,
    Reef heron, reef heron.
Your wings hasten, your beak hastens, your eyes hasten,
    Reef heron, reef heron.
Urem Tariga is first; others are behind.
Urem Tariga soars upwards like a bird.
It is a heron, a seagull."

After reaching the shore the heroes towed the log through the water to the workshop. At that stage Mafofo told his plans to the heroes in the rest of the villages of the Wonevaro and Bagiau districts, and they agreed to set about making their canoes. He refrained from approaching anyone from Takul, Bukdi, or Ga because these areas are on the weather side of the island, where the reef gives no protection from the heavy surf, and launching

The steersman.

a large craft would be impossible. Afterwards he and his companions shaped the log into a dugout. As soon as it was ready he carried out a rite to make the timber strong. He anointed it with coconut cream, and then he scrubbed the outside with a bundle of leaves of a certain species of plant mixed with the bark of a certain species of tree (both leaves and bark are notable for their rough, sandpapery texture and their toughness). Then he had the other men blacken its surface with burning pandanus leaves. Once they had finished he ensured that the completed vessel would not drift with the current but would always aim directly for the correct destination by washing the eyes of the figurehead and wiping them tenderly in a special way with soft bark-cloth.

So the building of *Urem Tariga* went on, with the carving of the hull and the collection of the timber for the wash strake, outrigger float, booms, and pegs, and of the creepers for lashing them all in place. At each step Mafofo carried out magic, and, as before, the spells and description of the rites are incorporated in the account when it is given in complete form. Finally, the day for the launching came, and still more magic was performed. By now the other canoes were also ready, and at the hour appointed by Mafofo the fleet assembled along the beach at Dap. The folk who were remaining behind stowed the cargo aboard and subsequently entertained the crews with a farewell dance. Mafofo's blood brother Wonka, from a village in the interior, led the festivities, and at their conclusion Mafofo entrusted the care of his wives and cultivations to him.

A recital of the incidents that took place on the expedition follows—where danger was averted and by what practical or magical means, the order of the ports of call, how the foreigners were encouraged to make exchanges, what were the specialities of each place, and so on.

At length, when the supply of Wogeo goods had been given away and preparations were in train for the return journey, Mafofo had a vivid dream. He saw his favorite wife and his brother Wonka conducting an affair, and the latter setting his seal upon the woman, with her full approval, by tattooing a design on her mons veneris. (The pair could reasonably have assumed Mafofo's continuing ignorance, for in normal circumstances a husband and his wife are never naked together.)

Mafofo determined to test the truth of the vision. As the canoes approached Dap and he saw the crowds assembling on the beach, he warned his crew that they must carry out his orders exactly.

The villagers splashed into the sea to their knees to haul the vessels ashore, and he then gave the word to push out once more. The result was that everyone in the welcoming party was dragged down and became wet to the waist. He watched the woman closely and, sure enough, observed how she winced as the water reached the spot where the scar of the tatoo was still not fully healed.

The following morning he asked her to accompany him so that they might look at the gardens together. He suggested intercourse as they walked through the forest, and when she submitted he seized the opportunity to make an exploration with his fingers for the marks. He took care to be so gentle that she remained unaware of what he was doing. Now positive of the couple's guilt, he wanted revenge. He was so fond of Wonka, however, that he felt a further test was necessary.

The initial step was the construction of a village clubhouse. The idea of such a structure had already occurred to a culture hero in another village, a fact that Mafofo freely acknowledged by following the procedures there laid down, but he made several innovations in both the order of the tasks and the ritual accompanying them, thereby setting precedents for the Dap residents of the future. When the building was almost complete he invited the inhabitants of each of the neighboring communities to the north and the south to adorn a post with their respective identifying carvings. These he examined closely, comparing them with the mental image, gathered through his finger tips, of that imprinted on his wife. All were different, so he obliterated them with a mixture of charcoal and the sticky sap of the breadfruit tree. Last he called in Wonka's group, and there before his eyes was what he had been seeking. "Enter," he begged the visitors, "and I will send my wife in with food for you to eat." The woman was unwilling to do his bidding, for elsewhere females were not permitted to go inside the club, but Mafofo insisted. Then he banged the door shut, barred it on the outside, and put a flaming torch to the walls. "Wonka, my blood brother," he called, "take this wife of mine for yourself. I give her to you, and the pair of you can bake together like joints of pork."

The imprisoned party began screaming with fear, but Wonka

comforted them with a promise to contrive their escape. He told the woman to grasp his bark corselet with both hands and the rest to make a line in single file behind her, each holding fast to the person in front. Then he recited a magical spell, and, behold! The smoke from the fire solidified into a rocky archway stretching from the club to Wonka's village. Over this they all passed unobserved by anyone from below. Mafofo, believing that he was avenged, composed a song of triumph: "Wonka, you are wet; we in Dap are dry; Wonka and his relatives are no more than cooks for us." Drums and gongs of rejoicing, however, soon began to sound in Wonka's home in the hills. Mafofo's mother, sent to investigate, reported that all had arrived back safely and were dancing to celebrate their deliverance.

That night Mafofo begged the residents of Job and Bariat to make an attack. They agreed; but one of their number despatched a message to his sister, who had married a follower of Wonka, warning her to find some excuse for paying a visit to another settlement. She disclosed the plan to her husband, who reported it to Wonka. Forearmed, he laid a trap. He and his men gathered huge boulders and balanced them at the edge of a precipice alongside the northern approach to the village. At a signal given by a sentry posted nearby, they rolled the rocks down on the raiders, forcing those who were not killed to retreat. An expedition from Kinaba and Mwarok to the south was repelled by similar tactics. The stones, lying in disorder as they fell, are visible to this day.

Next Mafofo turned to the inhabitants of the Bagiau district. They also agreed to help, but Wonka's supporters killed their two scouts, and the effort was equally unsuccessful. (One scout, a man, had grown bored and was masturbating—his semen became a deposit of white chalk—and the other, a woman, had allowed her attention to wander while she urinated—she left a waterfall behind.) On this occasion Wonka built four palisades, one inside the other, and constructed a fan-shaped spear-thrower that enabled his warriors to hurl spears in several directions simultaneously.

Wonka, although so consistently victorious, was by now weary of fighting. He assembled all his people, descended with them to the coast, took the canoes, and sailed to other lands, where today allegedly his escapades are still recalled in myths. His settlement

remained empty, and eventually, after the houses had fallen into
ruin, the forest reclaimed the site. Today human beings cultivate
Wonka's garden land, but nobody has ever wished to occupy his
village. The Dap householders adopted the Wonka design as their
own, nevertheless, and now carve it on houseposts, drums, and
canoes.

Mafofo, before his departure to another world with the rest of
the heroes, raised an upright block of basalt in front of his dwelling, where it has remained. The ancestors called it "Mafofo," the
name by which it is still known. At its feet several flat stones, each
representing a minor hero, are embedded in the ground in the
form of a crude pavement. The Dap headman who now owns
Mafofo's magic treats the obelisk with special respect, and every
smaller stone has an association with a particular family group.

Mafofo does not appear in any other myth, but a collection of
short tales tells of the doings of Wonka and his two foolish
younger brothers, Yabuk and Maguj. In one of them it is related
that Wonka pierced the trunk of a certain tree and from it obtained all the water his villagers required. Each time a vessel was
filled he took the greatest care in replacing the plug in the hole.
Then one day, busy with other work, he sent the two brothers to
replenish the bamboo containers. They did not understand and
cut the tree down instead of merely pulling out the bung. The
result was that in this part of the country the only water available
is down a deep well. Wonka, enraged, sent them to distant Bajor
to collect water from the only major stream on the island. Again
they displayed their stupidity by attempting to carry the liquid in
open taro leaves. They spilled some at Falala and at Mwarok,
where permanent springs are now to be found, and the remainder
near Dap, where there is a small brook. On another occasion,
when Wonka's household fire had gone out, he sent the two to
fetch a burning ember from a neighbor. They allowed the ember
to die, and in an endeavor to hide their negligence they disguised
the cold ashes with saliva, which was bright red from their having
chewed betelnut. Wonka threw the mess away, and from it red
ochre, used as a cosmetic, is obtained.

Today the Dap folk quote the main Mafofo-Wonka myth as
their authority for a headman of the settlement—in 1934 it was

Marigum—having the responsibility for deciding when trading voyages should be conducted and how they should be organized. This particular official, who has the hereditary right to occupy the house site beside the Mafofo stone, always inherits from his predecessor a full knowledge of the story and of the various magical canoe spells, and once he has given the word, the events follow in sequence precisely according to the traditional pattern, task upon task, rite upon rite. In this myth also is the warrant for the constructional work on the Dap clubhouse and the special features that characterize it, such as the obligatory attendance at one point of the women, who in every other village are forbidden to approach. Finally, the myth describes the punishment meted out to the adulterous couple. This description is often cited as reason enough for the condemnation of sexual affairs outside marriage.

There is also another myth telling how trading voyages began. This myth is the property of the people of Falala village in Bagiau district, who allege that it gives them the absolute right to conduct the expeditions. They insist on its genuineness and when by themselves accuse the Dap residents generally, and Marigum in particular, of wickedly twisting the Mafofo-Wonka story for the sake of Dap's aggrandizement. "Our heroes ordained that we should be first," they told me. "Dap can come along too, of course, but ought to be behind us, not in front." As often as I recounted such a remark my Dap neighbors dismissed it as preposterous. They asserted that theirs was the only authentic trading myth (*nanasa*) and that the other was a mere folktale (*sigilagila*) brought to Wogeo, probably in mangled form, from the island of Koil.[2] The inhabitants of Takul and Bukdi districts, who, because they take no part in arranging the journeys, might be expected to offer a disinterested opinion, are in fact influenced by their varying ties

[2]The situation resembles that of Roman Catholic and Protestant Churches arguing over ritual differences and basing respective claims on varying interpretations of disputed passages in the Vulgate. Thus in one text the Roman Catholics supported the reading *ipsa* and hence were able to attribute to the Virgin the crushing of the serpent of evil and heresy, whereas the Protestants supported the reading *ipse* and attributed the action to the Son. Pope Pius V (1566-1572) issued a Bull in an endeavor to reconcile the two points of view. The serpent, he said, was indeed crushed by the Virgin but with the aid of the Son—a statement that became the theme for the well-known painting in the Borghese collection by Caravaggio (see M. Calvesi, *Treasures of the Vatican* [London 1962], p. 187).

of kinship. Therefore, some side with Falala and some with Dap, and a small minority refuse to commit themselves. Yet everyone admits that as far back as he can recall from personal experience or hearsay Dap has exercised the privilege. The relevant point here, however, may well be the personality of Marigum, who has always been able to dominate the Falala headman Kaman, his exact contemporary. It seems possible that the more outstanding of the two leaders, whichever at any given time this happened to be, has taken the initiative, justifying the action by reference to his own myth while simultaneously denigrating that of the rival whom he has eclipsed.

Briefly, the second story, which Falala uses to support its claims, runs as follows. The culture hero Libwabwe, of Koil island, had an affair with the wife of his blood brother, Mwanubwa. Later, when Mwanubwa was erecting a clubhouse, he persuaded Libwabwe to go down into one of the postholes to perform magic to make the building secure. Then, as soon as the adulterer was below, he dropped an upright post on top of him and replaced the earth. But Libwabwe transformed himself into an insect (the name means "borer"), ate through the timber, and escaped. Mwanubwa then decided to drown him. He suggested that they each build a canoe for a voyage to Wogeo. As the more skilled shipwright, Mwanubwa offered to prepare his vessel first to serve as a model. He took care to fasten his outrigger float with tough creepers, but cleverly hid them under a cover of flimsy liana. Libwabwe assumed that this vine would be adequate, and when he put to sea his craft soon foundered. All save two members of his crew, who knew a magical spell to keep afloat, perished miserably. This pair were transformed into seagulls.

Mwanubwa sailed around Wogeo in search of a spot for a settlement. First he went along the exposed north coast. His aged mother was on board, and as he rounded one of the headlands she died. He went ashore to bury her and had already dug the grave before the local inhabitants chased him away. In anger he splashed with his paddle, causing great waves to crash on the rocks. That is why navigation on this side is hazardous. The canoe shook so violently in the storm that coals from the fire fell into the sea and drifted to the shore, giving rise to several hot springs. Eventually

Mwanubwa reached Falala and made it his home.

Time passed, the Canarium almond trees Mwanubwa had planted were flourishing, and his people had woven a store of fishing nets. He now had the idea of exchanging the surplus for items of overseas production. He invited the other Bagiau and Wonevaro villages to join him, and when preparations were complete the fleet of canoes set out. He had not yet buried his mother's body and now took it with him for disposal on the mainland. But the stench was so disgusting that the party forced him to abandon it at one of the first ports of call, a place named Kep. The decomposing flesh turned into the clay from which all the pots of the area are manufactured.

There is no need to relate Mwanubwa's further adventures, though it may be stated that these also bear a strong similarity to those of Mafofo. Each one provides the excuse for some variation of custom peculiar to Falala. Before his final disappearance Mwanubwa too erected a block of basalt, and alongside this his mortal successors, a line of headmen and their families, have consistently built their dwellings.

The Living Heroes

Last we have to consider the heroes who remained behind when the others left. Alone of all the spirits, these can intervene directly in human affairs. They are unique also in that, despite their names being known, their exploits are not related in a single myth. Yet, as with the heroes of the Mafofo and Mwanubwa type, they are represented by flat stones—the ones already mentioned that are embedded in the earth at the base of the columns. Today each household, or occasionally a group of households all closely related to one another, identifies itself with such a stone.

The significance of the living heroes is twofold. They are responsible for the magic that ordinary folk carry out to benefit their day-to-day concerns—rites to bring rain or sun, prolific harvests and annihilation of insect pests, satisfactory hauls of fish, illness of enemies and the recovery of kin, and so forth—and they also punish trespassers and hence give supernatural support to the system of land tenure.

Scattered over the island, half a dozen or more to the territory surrounding every village, are various spots held to be sacred. In most there is an element of danger or of the unusual. They include sink-holes in the limestone rock, pools where streams disappear underground, gloomy caverns, unexpected vertical cliffs, hot springs, and trees of enormous girth and height (mainly of Ficus species). Each is the dwelling place of a colony of living heroes, who have at times been seen in the vicinity masquerading either as humans or as snakes—not perhaps by anyone now alive, but by parents or grandparents recently deceased. If they appeared as men they were recognizable by their black skin, darker than that common in northern New Guinea, by their staring eyes, and by the profusion of their ornaments—circular boars' tusks, rattan armlets and wristbands with shell rings inserted in them, breast belts embroidered with small cowries, and towering headdresses of bird-of-paradise plumes—but when spoken to they quickly vanished. The snakes were also distinctive, with multicolored bands like a rainbow. There are even herds of heroic domestic pigs. You and I might think such animals wild, but to the owners they are tame. A hunter can tell a hero pig by its uncharacteristic behavior. If instead of running away it stands and confronts him, if it gores his dogs, or if after receiving a severe wound it still escapes, then clearly it is not a normal beast. Other people maintain that it is also identifiable by a scarlet hibiscus flower growing from its rump in place of a tail, but with this no hunter will agree.

Each hero develops a fellow feeling for the residents of the settlement in whose territory his own sacred home is situated. Though normally invisible, he watches them closely in the knowledge that the rights he himself once exercised have been so faithfully transmitted down the generations, and he has a sense of pride in the village as though they were his descendants. But they already possess his magic, and he has no power to give them any kind of practical help. His effort has to be confined to an endeavor to protect their property. So he and his companions watch out for any stranger proceeding inside the boundaries of the village lands without legitimate excuse. Single individuals, or a small group, the heroes strike down with sudden illness, but if a large party intrudes (perhaps in pursuit of a pig, or chasing after some of the local girls, or attempting to steal a basket of Canarium almonds) they signal the offense by sending a brief storm with lightning to destroy a fruit tree or a tree valued for its timber.

A person falling ill shortly after he has been guilty of trespassing summons any relatives who own garden plots in the vicinity of the area within which the misconduct occurred. He confesses and begs their intervention on his behalf. The senior of them promises to set the matter right and as soon after as possible marches off to one of the sacred spots of the village. He carries with him a collection of rubbish—perhaps a few cigarette butts, a package of vegetable peelings, or a bundle of areca-nut husks— and this he reverently lays on the ground as though it were an offering of great price, telling the heroes as he does so that it is a gift from the wrongdoer in expiation of the fault. He announces also that the man is sorry, that little damage or harm resulted, and that he himself, the speaker, bears no animosity and hopes that they will relent. Recovery is accepted as proof of forgiveness, continuation of the disease as evidence of mistaken diagnosis and incorrect treatment—the patient must have been the target of human ill will and thus a victim of sorcery. There is never any thought of making a sacrifice of goods of real worth. According to most people, the heroes have all they need, and the gesture of contrition suffices; but there are a few who maintain instead that the heroes are simpleminded and so readily fooled.

Conclusion

The beliefs we have been discussing have the effect of providing an ultimate validity—what Malinowski would have called a charter[3]—for the norms of conduct. They are a dogmatic assertion that custom, far from originating in the fumblings of ordinary behavior, flows directly from divine inspiration. Accepted morality is right not on account of logic or rationality, but because this is what the culture heroes laid down as correct before antiquity began. Failure to conform is therefore tantamount to sacrilege. A comparison might be made with the Jewish faith in the presenta-

[3]See B. Malinowski, *Myth in Primitive Psychology* (London 1926), pp. 23, 38; and *A Scientific Theory of Culture* (North Carolina 1944), pp. 48 ff., III, 140, 162.

tion to Moses of the tablets of stone, and with that of the Christians in the Crucifixion and Resurrection. In Wogeo also the voice of men has been translated into the word of God and hence beyond cavil or criticism.

The myths of the heroes give justification for the people's occupation of the island and their extreme ethnocentrism as well as warrant for the practices that they all share and for those that are monopolized by particular groups, for the allocation of the rights to land, and for the special privileges of the various households. Here, too, is the sanction for the ownership of the systems of magic and testimony of their efficacy. Finally, the myths give practical directions for a number of technical processes, such as the construction of canoes and the routing of trading voyages.

III   The Spirit World

The Souls of the Dead

The souls of the dead (*mariap*) form a second class of supernatural beings. They have little bearing on human affairs and need not delay us long. Their origin is to be sought in the spiritual essence peculiar to living persons and manifest in the shadow (*vanunu*). Ordinarily, the substance is enclosed within one's physical body, though it can, of its own accord, leave him temporarily during the night, thereby giving rise to dreams; or it may be stolen, a misfortune that leads to illness. Only with death does the essence achieve independence. At first, bewildered by the metamorphosis, the soul desires to stay in the familiar surroundings, and the mourners have to drive it away. Weeping, it journeys to a rocky headland on the northeast corner of the island and thence climbs a ridge leading to the mountains in the center, where the afterworld is located. This afterworld remains its home forever, except that at intervals, when overcome with nostalgia, it descends in the form of a firefly to its old haunts. In Melanesia these insects are commonly—though not universally—associated with spirits. Often they are feared, but in Wogeo they are not. A man on whose hand a firefly has alighted brushes it off with only the mildest show of repugnance.

Most people also maintain that the soul has the power to materialize as a ghost and frighten householders by, for instance, standing in dark corners, banging doors, or knocking articles from shelves. Others, a minority, protest that such a visible spirit is derived from a different kind of essence that reveals itself during the individual's life in his image in a pool of water or, nowadays, in a looking glass.

The afterworld is rarely a topic of spontaneous conversation, but the men may advance views on the subject in response to an enquiry. The few whose essences have, for one reason or another, actually visited the place put forward their opinions most clearly. Thus my neighbor Kalal one night dreamed that the soul of his brother, killed in an accident only a few weeks earlier, had seized him in its arms and carried him by a secret route into the company of the departed. Fortunately the multitude of these beings were able to tell from his body odor that he was still alive, and they compelled the offending soul to release him. But by then he had already seen much of what was going on. The souls of females, he explained, pass through an initiation ceremony resembling that performed on earth for growing youths. Their status is thereby enhanced, and they are able to take a place equivalent to that of the souls of the males. Both male and female souls spend their time much as mortals do, though their activities are less satisfying. They cultivate the soil, tend pigs, and go fishing, but their skin never glows with sweat; they cook and eat, but their food lacks flavor; they copulate, but no child is ever born to them; and they quarrel and fight, but they cannot slay one another. "Yet there they are," Kalal concluded. "I know, I know truly from having seen them, that nobody has ever perished even if death has brought about changes."

Generally a question about the influence that the souls may have on human affairs meets with the response that the dead can do no more than steal a person's spiritual essence in the hope of thereby removing him to their own land of shadows. The most malicious and spiteful are those of men murdered during a raid and those of women lost in childbirth (the bodies of such folk have to be buried in the bush, not under the house, the customary spot for the grave). But even these souls are powerless to do permanent damage to an adult. A mature person deprived of part of himself loses consciousness—that is to be expected—and he may even rave in delirium, but the condition is speedily remedied by the administration of a dish of the hot vegetable curry known as *sur* (as we shall see presently, a patient seriously ill is described as "cold" although his temperature may be above normal). If after the relatives have forced the food down his throat he still fails to respond, it is assumed that the symptoms must have been wrongly identified. A sorcerer may be blamed and other medicaments tried. It follows that grownups have no fears for themselves; yet they admit to serious concern for the children, who are not strong enough to withstand severe shock. Magical protection may be sought, but the infant-mortality rate is high, and many ailments that to us would be trivial often prove fatal. At such times, although the parents are at first apt to attribute the death to the black arts of an enemy and clamor for aid in taking revenge, the bulk of the population is content to accuse the souls, a reaction that has the comforting effect of absolving them from the dangerous obligation to pick a human culprit.

Certain practices suggest a hope, nevertheless, that the souls may be able to impinge on everyday events. Thus a person performing magic follows up the recitation of the spell by naming those of his forebears who possessed the requisite knowledge. He is not convinced of the consequent cooperation of their souls in achieving the end desired, but the chances are that he will say in explanation that he makes the appeal "just in case." Again, people engaged in a hazardous enterprise, such as raiding a hostile settlement or sailing on a voyage overseas, seem to gain confidence from carrying a collection of the bones of deceased kinsfolk, especially if these had been socially prominent. Within a year or so of the funeral of a headman or famous warrior, after a sufficient interval has elapsed for the decomposition of the body, the son has the duty of disinterring the phalanges, ulnae, clavicles, and mandible. The last he retains himself, but the rest he distributes. The recipient stores his relics in the clubhouse, taking them out only for special undertakings, when he wears them attached to a necklace or wristband. Like the magician, he admits the lack of a dogma about ghostly assistance and argues simply that the remains give him comfort. Some men even confessed to me that in extreme danger they had clutched the bones and prayed aloud to the souls for rescue.

Mask Spirits and Flute Spirits

People speak freely about a third type of supernatural beings, the spirit monsters, and even describe their appearance, but the men when by themselves deny that such creatures exist. Their argument is that, as monsters must always be impersonated, they are to be regarded by the initiated as figments of the culture heroes' imagination, a deliberate invention whose dual purpose is to facilitate the accumulation of food before a feast or a distribution and to serve as a means of keeping the women in their proper place. Yet despite such statements, when the occasion calls for the presence of the monsters, the behavior of both sexes seems to indicate unquestioning belief. Not only do mothers hustle the children into the house, but the male actors taking part submit to numerous ritual restrictions.

Spirit monsters are of two kinds, the *lewa* (also the word for "mask") and the *nibek* (also meaning "flute"). The former are primarily associated with the lesser food distributions (*walage*) held for the residents of a single district, the latter with the elaborate festivals (*warabwa*) in which the guests come from different parts of the island. Each type includes those from the bush (*kwab*) and those from the village (*malal*). The arrival of bush *lewa* places a ban on the collection of certain bush crops, notably Tahitian chestnuts; of bush *nibek* on picking such orchard products as bananas and areca nuts; of village *lewa* on gathering ripe coconuts; and of village *nibek* on killing domestic pigs.

Usually the main feature of the impersonation consists of imitating the voices of the monsters with musical instruments—bullroarers (*mumumu*) for the bush *lewa*, leaf whistles and bamboo trumpets (*wakaka* and *muna* respectively) for the bush *nibek*, and bamboo flutes for the village *nibek*. The village *lewa* are the sole exception. These are represented by masked dancers (*tangbwal*) wearing tall headdresses and long garments of dyed fibers. A headman, on reaching a decision about the organization of a food distribution, performs the ceremony to conjure up the monsters appropriate to the importance of the distribution, and his followers then, according to requirements, either make off for the forest twirling bullroarers or blowing whistles and trumpets or stay near the village piping on flutes or prancing in fancy dress. To begin with, only the residents of the headman's housing cluster perform, but later on all his kinsmen take part. On occasion, too, when a heavy task has to be carried out, the headman announces informally that with monsters on hand the work will be less arduous. So the hum of bullroarers regulates the efforts of the gang employed to haul logs for a canoe down the mountainside, and the booming of trumpets provides the rhythm for the laborers erecting the frame of a large building. He may also use the monsters, again with a preliminary ceremony, to add to his own dignity or to emphasize the status of his fellow officeholders. He has the right to order flutes or masks for family celebrations, such as those at the first menstruation of one of his daughters, and flutes to express sympathy with another leader who has suffered sudden misfortune, perhaps illness or an accident.

To avoid repetition I shall confine my account to the details of the village *lewa* and the village *nibek.*

Village *Lewa*

A headman intending to hold an intradistrict food distribution fixes the day, about a week ahead, for summoning a village *lewa*, a *tangbwal,* from the world of the spirits. The interval gives the men time to collect a set of fiber skirts from their wives. The theory is that the women are in ignorance of what is proposed, but most husbands talk freely about the plan. Indeed, it is difficult to see how they could obtain the clothing otherwise.

Late in the afternoon of the day agreed upon, the men and youths of the cluster, with one or two close relatives from other places, drift along to the area on the beach where traditionally all spirit monsters make their first appearance. Once everybody is present the lads start blowing leaf whistles, the signal for the women to call the children inside and bar the doors. Meantime a young man, when possible somebody with histrionic talent, retires into the trees and, with the help of a couple of companions, dresses up in the skirts. Some he ties around his shoulders to hide pads on his chest and abdomen, and on his head he twists a sheet of the spathe of a wild palm, making a cap to resemble that worn

Masks worn by *lewa* monsters.

by a person in a state of taboo (see below p. 84).

Immediately after the sun has sunk below the horizon, the headman advances towards the water's edge and calls in turn the names of a series of female village *lewa*. Every place has its own, but he begins with that of Ga, where, according to the origin myth, the culture heroes initiated the custom. At his side stand two assistants, often his sons, and as he reaches the name of the female *lewa* of his own settlement, asking, "Come, are you So-and-so?" one of them strikes a hand drum while the other smashes a green coconut so that the operator can take a mouthful of the liquid and spray it over the assembled gathering. The man in skirts now wades into the sea to one side of the crowd, and the assistants score a groove, as of the keel of a canoe, in the sand or pebbles. He emerges in the center of this grove, obliterating his footprints as he does so lest the women should recognize them. The female *lewa* has arrived!

The recitation of the names is modeled on the procedure for an infant.[1] A senior relative goes through the list of the child's ancestors and living kinsmen until the appellation already selected has been reached, when, similarly, assistants sound a drum and crack a coconut open. The idea seems to be that a linkage should be demonstrated between the youngster and his various cognates, first those of the past, then those of the present.

The same kind of ceremony marks the summoning of any of the other spirit monsters and also the inauguration of a new club, a great house for a headman, or a trading canoe. Myths relate how each of these phenomena was started in a particular village either on Wogeo or another island of the Schouten group—one in Maluk village, one in Dap village, one in the island of Blupblup, and so forth. The recital always begins with the place of origin and then gives the names of all the monsters, clubhouses, or whatever it may be from the intervening settlements. Thus today is tied to yesterday and simultaneously a reminder is given of the cultural homogeneity of the archipelago.

In the gathering dusk, after the arrival of the *lewa*, a procession advances towards the clubhouse: first the headman, next the youths blowing their whistles, then the monster simulating—to much laughter—the heavy gait of a woman far advanced in pregnancy, and finally the rest of the crowd. They mount the ladder and go inside. Instantly the whistles cease, and soon the housewives bring across steaming bowls of vegetable curry, the delicacy always served to the sick and to those in a condition of ritual danger. The men accept the food on behalf of the *lewa* but consume it themselves.

Another delay follows until the monster's delivery is due. This is the time for making the garments for her expected offspring. I have described elsewhere how the right to cultivate a particular

[1] I. Hogbin, "A New Guinea Infancy," *Oceania*, Vol. 13 (1942-1943), p. 293.

set of gardening blocks carries with it the duty of fixing a certain rafter when the roof is built for a new clubhouse.[2] The different parts of the costumes are similarly associated with the club, and land, rafter, and *lewa* adornments all go together. The householders who till the soil of blocks we may call A not only have to lash rafter A_1 in place, but also furnish skirt fringe A_2 or possibly a pair of sleeves. The throat fringes, embroidered with rows of small cowrie shells, and the headpiece must always come from the headman. Much of the actual labor is the women's responsibility, though the men always help.

The first job is to prepare a quantity of sago-leaf fiber, which has to be boiled with vegetable dyes. After drying, the fiber is plaited on cords and cut to the right length. Meantime other workers sew a corselet and sleeves from palm spathes and weave a giant version of the normal headdress of the mature man—a wicker cone upwards of two feet in length but open at both ends. They stick tufts of their own hair over the smaller hole and at the other fix a black wooden mask, sometimes left plain, sometimes painted with streaks and circles in white clay and yellow ochre. Each headman inherits a couple of such masks from his predecessors; they are of similar general design except that the shape and length of the nose differs. The older specimens, carved before the introduction of steel tools, are artistically superior to the newer substitutes.

The full dress of a male village *lewa* consists of the wooden mask and wicker headdress adorned with dogs' teeth, circular boars' tusks, strips of possum fur, bird-of-paradise skins, and other ornamental feathers—finery lent by the headman, the cluster residents, and well-wishers from places nearby—the sleeved bodice, and six to eight red-brown fringes reaching from the chin to the ground. With all this goes a handrattle of dried bean pods and a palmwood spear banded with cassowary feathers.

The workers while making the costumes submit to taboos to ensure the success of the later celebrations. They partake of nothing before the evening meal, which they are obliged to eat outside

[2] I. Hogbin and P. Lawrence, *Studies in New Guinea Land Tenure* (Sydney 1966) pp. 40-4.

the house, preferably on the beach, and always in daylight; they
avoid sexual intercourse; and they refrain from visiting other set
tlements. To secure a good deep color for the fibres in the skirts
they also chew large quantities of betelnut during the dyeing
process.

Every headman owns a pair of male-*lewa* names, one for each
of his two masks, and usually the mother *lewa* produces twins,
who receive their designation with the normal drum-and-coconut
ritual. I have never seen more than this number, but occasionally,
when the two headmen of the village are on especially good terms
and have decided to sponsor the distribution jointly, there may be
quadruplets. The men inform the women that the birth has taken
place, and one of their number, disguised as the female *lewa*, limps
to the beach for water to wash the offspring. Afterwards the
women again bring curry. But, although male *lewa* are born fully
grown, they do not descend from the club till next day. That
afternoon the headman hangs from one of his verandah posts a
spray of white unbroken coconut leaflets plaited in a special way
to indicate the type of food now forbidden.

Early in the morning the youths and younger men cut a pile
of palm leaves to stand against the edge of the roof of the clubhouse and thus shield the space underneath from public view.
Here the men of the cluster gather with hand drums and a
wooden slit gong and begin practicing dance tunes. Soon the
costumes are assembled, and two (or four) of the crowd volunteer
to give the first performance. Rarely a third offers to represent the
mother, but as a rule she seems from this point to be forgotten.

The dancers push through the screens and take up positions
facing one another, each with a rattle in one hand and a spear in
the other. A chorus begins to the beat of the drums and gong, and
they take up the rhythm. They crook their legs, push their buttocks out, and shuffle to and fro, advancing and retreating, whirl-
ing and turning, dipping under one another's waving arms, and
clashing their rattles together. But they make no speech sounds,
for they are supposed to be dumb. The song rises in a crescendo,
and faster and faster they go till it appears that only a miracle can
keep the nodding headdresses in place. Within about twenty min-

utes they retire exhausted, and there is a pause while they undress and other men take over.

The show goes on in this fashion throughout the day. Not till the later part of the afternoon do the women pay much attention. Earlier they will have been bringing in vegetables from the gar-

The *lewa* monsters dancing.

dens and getting ready for a heavier meal than is usual. But once the food is safely in the pot they don their best fiber skirts—bleached snow white or dyed in alternate bands of saffron and vermillion or crimson and dark brown—and move in small groups to the dance area in front of the club. By now many of the men also are resplendent with hair the color of henna, and with white, yellow, or red pigment on their faces. Some of the drummers may come into the open, and if so the women dance with shuffling movements at the edge of the circle, while the young boys imitate the actions of the *lewa* figures as best they can.

At length, round about sunset, the costumes go back into the club, and the musicians hang their drums in the rafters. Dinner is served, and, in high spirits, all partake with keen appetite.

The collection of ripe coconuts is now banned. They fall to the ground and are left undisturbed until the distribution, which coincides with the departure of the *lewa*. The oily cream extracted from the grated meat of ripe coconuts, in Melanesian societies the principal source of fat, is an important ingredient of most culinary delicacies. The prohibition thus has the same kind of effect as would be achieved in our society by a restriction for a period on the sale of butter and edible oils to allow for the building up of stocks in storage. The embargo is not reinforced by ritual sanctions, and failure to respect it is never thought to lead to supernatural punishment. What does happen is that the headman closes the dance area by fixing crossed spears in the center to indicate that "the *lewa* are asleep." The area remains in this state until the culprit admits his fault and presents the people with special food, usually the carcass of a pig, as a form of atonement.

Breaches are difficult to discover, and, ostensibly to keep watch, from time to time pairs of older youths put on the *lewa* costumes and wander through the orchards and gardens. Their real purpose, however, is to have a game. They sneak up quietly near any women or lads working in small parties and spring upon them from behind, perhaps brandishing canes, perhaps attempting no more than to tickle them. The victims may not be aware of the exact identity of their assailant, but even the least sophisticated know that he can only be a neighbor in disguise. Yet they utter piercing shrieks, and many lose control of the bladder or bowels in their terror. They seem to be consciously shutting off their reasoning powers to have fun, for when discussing the incident afterwards they roar with laughter. Here is a New Guinea equivalent of our Dracula novels and Frankenstein-monster films.

The pulsating of Wogeo percussion instruments, hand drum and slit gong, is to European ears less appealing than the plaintive call of a bamboo flute; but, coming over the foothills and along the beaches, it is to the people wildly exciting. The inhabitants of the other villages in the district find the steady thumping almost irresistible, and they would join in at once did not etiquette forbid their attendance on the first day. The headman's relatives from each settlement must make a formal visit as a group before individuals feel at liberty to attend by themselves. The leaders decide on a convenient time and send word beforehand so that the hosts may be ready. Householders of importance make certain that their wives bring a basket of food to help out with the entertainment, but nobody need be ashamed of coming empty-handed.

The party of guests arrives in midmorning, and immediately a pair take the *lewa* costumes and start dancing. For an hour or two the local men provide the orchestra while their own womenfolk mingle with the visitors as spectators. But at noon or soon afterwards the hosts are obliged to leave. They walk to the gardens and orchards, bring back food and extra ingredients for the betelnut mixture, and during the late afternoon cook a big meal, which they share out. The youths and men, guests and hosts, adjourn to the club, and the women and children scatter among the dwellings.

Once each of the clusters in the district has done this honor to the headman who called up the *lewa*, anyone can spend an afternoon dancing as he feels inclined. Celebrations do not take place every day. Gardening, fishing, and the multitude of other ordinary tasks have still to be carried out. The average frequency is perhaps once per week for a morning-to-evening effort and twice more during the week for an hour or two before sundown. The headman himself never takes the lead but lets his sons or nephews make the arrangements. He and the other elders also abstain from dressing up and dancing, not for reasons of dignity but because the exercise is so strenuous that they can no longer show to advantage. Sometimes they hold a drum or set to striking a gong, though in the main they prefer to be spectators. An especially good performance calls forth their applause. "*Wa, wa, wa . . .*," they shout, giving the name of the *lewa* concerned. A headman seldom rewards one of his own followers, but sometimes he may give a bird-of-paradise skin or a shell armlet to others who notably distinguish themselves.

After about three or four months, when a sufficient quantity of coconuts is available, the headman announces the date for the dispatch of the *lewa* back to the spirit world and, incidentally, the distribution. Doubtless he is influenced by the fact that the villagers may be approaching boredom with the dancing and the enforced stodgy diet. I shall describe the departure ritual that I witnessed in Dap a few weeks after my taking up residence there. The headman Marigum had summoned the *lewa* so that, as he said, he could reward his people for the hardship they had undergone during some of the initiation rites of one of his sons.

For several days each of the youths and younger men when returning from working in the gardens brought back a stout pole or a bundle of creepers, which he left on a pile close to the club. Eventually Marigum gave the word, and they began to erect a platform at the eastern edge of the settlement. This platform rested on a triangular frame that was a foot from the ground at the end facing the dance area and nine feet high at the other. The platform itself was fifteen feet long but no more than two feet wide. Around it ran a hand rail, and to this the workers tied hundreds of coconut leaflets rendered pliant by the removal of the midrib. The resulting low curtain they decorated with swags or orange and red fruits, garlands of crimson Cordyline leaves, and sprays of delicate yellow and pink Croton.[3] The structure was referred to as "the canoe" (*kat*) and represented the craft that was

[3]The ritual use throughout the Pacific of Cordyline, wrongly identified in some of the literature as Dracaena, is probably to be accounted for in part by the red color of the leaves. These are visible from a long distance against the dark green of the forest and can also be identified with blood. Leenhardt pointed out that the plant is long-lived, dry, and wiry and hence often represents the male element. Apparently unaffected by time and fire, it is the symbol of the permanence of the social group. See M. Leenhardt, "Le Ti," *Journal de la Société des Oceanists*, Vol. 2 (1946), p. 192.

to bear the *lewa* on their homeward journey to the land of the spirits. With a little imagination it could be pictured as riding before the crest of an advancing wave.

During the final afternoons all the inhabitants of the Wonevaro district came to Dap as a matter of course, and everyone who wished to do so had a turn dancing. Then the last day was upon us. The crowd began assembling at 3 o'clock, both sexes in their newest clothing and wearing ornaments. The men retired behind the screens below the club, leaving the women in the open. Half a dozen of the most skilful players took up a drum each, and the rest formed up with their hands on one or other of two long ropes of plaited stalks of ginger. At a given signal from an elder closely related to Marigum the two files emerged singing, with the drummers madly gyrating as they ran up and down between. Round and round the houses they went, fast at first and later more sedately. Soon many of the girls and even older women joined in at the sides. They were in pairs or in fours, each set with arms linked behind. Forwards and backwards they danced, singing all the time, with monotonous slouching steps. This continued till the sun was low in the sky. Then some youths slipped away to the club and blew a blast on their leaf whistles. At once the women began crying in a mournful long-drawn-out melody. Holding the children close, they ran into the houses, where they continued their keening.

Again the whistles sounded, and the men stepped into two rows, facing each other, thereby forming a broad pathway from the club to the canoelike platform. At a third whistle a wild yell burst from behind the club, and a small group of seniors pranced on the scene, each apparently in a transport of rage. The pair in front carried lighted torches of dried coconut leaves, and, gnashing their teeth and spitting mouthfuls of chewed ginger, they pushed the flames under the thatched eaves of the houses and into every dark corner. Behind them others bore spears and arrows, which they shot high over the rooftops. The purpose of this pantomime was to drive away any ghosts that may have been attending the *lewa*. Last to appear were the *lewa* themselves, impersonated by middle-aged men. This time they had strips of bark cloth some two fathoms long attached to their headdresses

—streamers that would float behind in the wind as the spirits flew on their journey. Immediately the watchers along the pathway stamped their left feet, turned outwards to the left, and threw themselves flat on the ground. The *lewa* strode between the prostrate bodies, mounted the platform, turned—in this case to the right—to face the west, and cast their arms aloft, catching the last rays of the setting sun with breathtaking theatrical effect. Now the whistles blew a fourth and last time. The men arose from the ground and helped their *lewa* companions to disrobe. The costumes they placed over a pair of light cane frames on the platform, giving as lifelike an impression as possible. At the stern of the canoe (the high end) they also fixed a paddle. The women now descended from the dwellings.

The *lewa* dummies remained in position for two or three days. Eventually members of Marigum's family removed the orna-

Dance preceding the dispatch of the *lewa* monsters.—Some of the men are playing hand-drums.

ments for return to their owners; unlashed the masks, which they hung in the club; tore the head cone and fringes in twain; dismantled the platform; and threw the debris into the bush immediately behind the club, where all relics of ritual paraphernalia are left to rot. The spot is held to be spiritually dangerous and is normally avoided. Those who must perforce enter are taboo and are obliged to take precautions before returning to ordinary life.

By now it was growing dark, but the distribution had still to take place. Before long people were kindling fires and lighting torches to see what they were doing.

Preparations had been going on during the morning for a few days previously. The Dap folk from the two clusters had collected their ripe coconuts from under the trees and gathered green coconuts for drinking. Marigum's household supplied 100 ripe nuts and 50 green nuts, and each of the remaining households, a dozen in all, supplied between 30 and 50 ripe nuts and about 20 green nuts. Thus the totals for the village were approximately 600 and 300 respectively. A group of men had also gone fishing. They had pooled their catch and, to preserve the fish, smoked it on a low frame over a slow fire. Then there was a store of sago starch, much of it provided by Marigum, and several giant taro corms, some weighing nearly 50 pounds. Under Marigum's directions the youths and younger men set all this food out on coconut-leaf mats, which they spread on the ground in rows in front of his house. The eight headmen of the four neighbouring villages then instructed their followers to add the contributions they were making. Each place had brought about a quarter of the amount given by the Dap residents. This made the grand totals 1200 ripe coconuts, 600 green coconuts, 60 pounds of dried fish, plus sago starch and taro—all from a district with a population, including infants, or less than 300.

Marigum directed one of his nephews to divide the food among the different villages. Every care had to be taken to see that nobody received any item that he had himself brought. Each set of villagers carried the baskets home, and here their headmen allocated portions among the households. Visitors received a little more than they had brought, hosts a little less. After a meal the people everywhere in the district spent a couple of hours before

The house of the headman Marigum in Dap village.—A distribution of coconuts and Pacific chestnuts is in progress.

retiring singing mournful songs to express sorrow for the departure of the *lewa*.

To the superficial observer the final proceedings, in a sense the basis for the entire affair, might have appeared not only an anticlimax but also a ridiculous waste of time and effort. People carried their supplies in some instances for over two miles, watched them being arranged on mats, then received the equivalent back again, and in the end shouldered the loads for an equally long walk home. But to those taking part the show was ample compensation. They were excited by the food and delighted to be handling it. "You Europeans look on provisions as something just to stuff your insides with, but to us in Wogeo they are for display and admiration as well. They are twice as important to us as to you," one of my friends explained. The opportunity for overeating is also a theme for pleasurable anticipation, despite the frequent painful after-effects.[4]

[4]For a fuller discussion on attitudes to food distributions see I. Hogbin and P. Lawrence, *Studies in New Guinea Land Tenure* (Sydney 1966), pp. 89, 90.

Village *Nibek*

The village *nibek*, often described as "the big things" or "the hidden things," are regarded as the most important of the monsters. Ordinarily their presence imposes a ban on the slaughter of pigs, and, as was mentioned, they are summoned as an essential prelude to the great interdistrict *warabwa* festivals. Such celebrations take place on a variety of occasions. Thus they are indispensable after the completion of a new club building or the construction of a large dwelling for a headman and when a headman formally appoints his heir. A headman can also organize a festival as a sort of potlatch to humble a rival from another part of the island. He has the right to call up the *nibek* when a major event takes place within his own family or when sympathy is due to a leader suffering from some misfortune, though at these times the *nibek* are in the village for only a few days, and the provision of pork is not necessarily a consideration.

When in mixed company the men describe the *nibek* as having a head like a snake's, a body like a huge stone, and legs like a centipede's. The mouth in repose, they say, is about the size of a human being's, though it can be expanded in the manner of a python swallowing a rat. In private they agree that, of course, the creatures are imaginary, with flutes to represent their voices. They then add that the women are completely fooled.

How far the females are really duped is difficult to assess. The young married housewives may accept without question what they are told, but I am not sure about their seniors. None of them was prepared to take me into her confidence, though one or two dropped a broad hint. My impression is that they are aware of much that goes on, if not the whole of it, but prefer to let the men continue assuming their ignorance. This feeling is confirmed by the ceremonies to celebrate a girl's first menstruation. Much of what takes place then seems to follow, and even imitate, the events during the initiation of the youths, when the flutes are in constant evidence. In my mind's eye—I emphasize that this is something I did not witness—I can see these older women clicking their tongues as they remark to one another about their husbands, "Poor fellows! Still, we'd better let them have their little games and not make them ashamed by laughing."

The flutes consist of the internode of a bamboo with the termi
nals pierced and a small square hole for blowing cut out a couple
of inches from the end. They vary in length from three to five feet
and always go in pairs—one, called the male (*nat*), from six to nine
inches longer than the other, the female (*veini*). Usually they are
decorated with feathers, dogs' teeth, and bands of rattan, small
cowrie shells, or fur. Every headman owns several pairs, each with
a name (Marigum's are called Manam Sakur, Maloa, and Makusa
—all words with no other meaning), and on any given occasion he decides which are to be used. Listeners, including the
women, can easily tell them apart by the difference in the
sounds.

Despite the prevalence of boring insects, a flute generally lasts
for a decade or longer. The appropriate variety of bamboo does
not grow locally, and when an instrument is showing signs of
wear the headman takes it with him on a trading voyage so that
he can seek a matching stem elsewhere. He may have a lucky find
on the mainland, but the chances are that he will be forced to look
in either Blupblup or Kadovar, two other islands in the Schouten
group. On returning home he fashions the new flute on the pattern of the old one, which he throws into the bushes behind the
club. It is on record that headmen have cut and named bamboos,
thereby "giving birth" to a pair, but this has happened only when
an eldest daughter was betrothed to an established leader and the
father wished to augment her dowry. He did not inform her of
the gift but handed it directly to the husband to hold in trust for
the heir, the woman's eldest son.

In giving a performance the two players face one another, the
man with the male flute holding it in the left hand, the one with
the female holding his in the right. They slowly revolve in a
clockwise direction, the former proceeding forward, the latter
backward, beating time with the free hand on the thigh as they
go. The tunes are mainly traditional—though occasionally a com-
poser may be inspired and dream a new one—but some flautists
are gifted with a more limpid tone than others. The Dap villagers
were always asking me to play a record of the Mozart oboe quartet
K.370, with Leon Goossens, who they said resembled Tafalti, one

Playing the flutes, which represent the voices of the *nibek* monsters.

of Marigum's sons, the local star. "You can't hear him breathing either!" they would say in admiration.

Drums and gongs may also be employed to mark the rhythm, but the most common accompaniment is a sounding board, "the *nibek's* bone" (*kalajong*), a piece of hardwood some three feet long and a couple of inches thick tapering from a width of six inches

to a point. The player holds it in his left hand and strikes the edge
with a short drumstick held in the right.[5]

Flautists and bone players receive regular magical potions from
the headman to maintain their strength, but after even a single
day's performance they must refrain from contact with the opposite sex and from smoking until the next new moon. When the
nibek are to be present over a long period, most youths and young
men consider the price too great for them to take part for more
than a month at a time. They join in for three or four weeks and
then spend an interval living normally before again coming forward.

I was present only once, in Gol village, for the arrival of the
nibek. The ceremony (unlike that for the *lewa*, which takes place
at dusk) is always performed before dawn. The men assembled at
the appropriate spot on the beach, two of them carrying the flutes
concealed in a basket; a third, the headman's assistant—on this
occasion a nephew—holding the usual green coconut for the naming ceremony; and a fourth bearing aloft the sounding board. It
is almost unthinkable that any female would have been abroad at
such an hour, but as a warning some youths set up a series of light
barricades of upright sticks interlaced with red Cordyline leaves.
When all was ready the headman picked up the butt of a palm leaf
and struck it hard against a rock. "Come, *nibek*," he called; then
after a moment's pause, "You are So-and-so," naming a pair from
Maluk village, the birthplace of the culture hero who first brought
the instruments to Wogeo. Other names followed, each preceded
by the blow on the rock, until he reached the pair he wanted.
Immediately the assistant broke his coconut, and the flautists
played a characteristic short trill. Afterwards one of those present
scraped the pebbles aside to leave a mark as of the beaching of a
canoe.

A procession now formed and marched to the village. At the
head was the sounding-board player, who struck the wood continuously; then, in order, several youths with baskets of sand,
which they scattered in handfuls as though it were falling from the
feet of the monsters; a party of torchbearers; nine men, in three

[5]Sounding boards are peculiar to Wogeo and not found elsewhere in the
region.

sets of three, brandishing spears; the bulk of the company; and
finally the flautists and the headmen. They advanced solemnly,
stamping regularly with the right foot until it seemed that the
forest was swaying and the earth shaking from the sound. Round
the village they went in a clockwise direction (that is, turning to
the right) and so one by one up the ladder and into the club. It
was now just daylight, and the women rose to cook the curry.
When the food was ready they called out, and some youths came
and carried it to the assembly. (Individual villages have their own
variations of the ceremonial, and in Dap the women go right
inside the clubhouse with the bowls—the only settlement, and
almost the only circumstance, in which females are allowed to
approach the sacred precinct.) As it happened, the Gol interdistrict *warabwa* festival was a potlatch and not associated with replacing the club, but when a new one of these is contemplated the
men take the flutes to the headman's house, which the women will
have temporarily vacated.

A few short trills were heard during the rest of the day, but
full-scale performances did not begin until the following morning.
There are several secluded groves on the headlands and in the
valleys of the foothills, and a small party set out for the one
selected for this occasion with the flutes and sounding board.
Later, as is customary, they played at daybreak, before regular
gardening tasks had begun, and at the close of the afternoon, when
work was finished. For some weeks the sounds were heard daily,
but after about a month once or twice a week sufficed.

Preparations for a festival take well over a year to complete.
Not only do the pigs have to be husbanded and fattened, but large
areas of ground must be cleared for the many extra gardens. If
there is to be a fresh club or a dwelling for the headman, construction is postponed till the people feel certain that the food will be
ready. Even then, during these final months, the work proceeds
intermittently so that plenty of time will be left for the other tasks.
The villagers pick out trees for the hardwood posts and stumps,
haul them to the settlement, shape them, and fix them in position.
Next come the ridge and side poles, the bearers and the joists, the
battens and the rafters. The palmwood flooring follows, and afterwards the sago-leaf thatch, which is always much thicker for a

clubhouse or a headman's dwelling than for an ordinary house. Clubs stand high off the ground, with the walls hidden behind the eaves, and painting the palm spathes lashed along the sides would therefore be pointless. But often carvings of men and beasts adorn the gable ends. The headman's dwelling, on the other hand, is raised up only the normal distance, from three to five feet, and as the walls are exposed, they make a fine surface for those with a flair for mural decoration. The designs are semiabstract, with red and yellow ochre, soot, and white pipeclay employed as pigments. Usually this building also has statues fixed to the gables. The favorite theme is a man with an enormous penis fully erect. The final adornments for both club and dwelling consist of festoons for the edge of the roof made from strings of white shredded coconut leaf and garlands of brightly colored fruit. Once these decorations are in position balsa-wood models of birds, fish, and coconuts are suspended from long flexible saplings fixed to the ends of the ridge pole. The naming ceremony now proceeds with the accustomed ritual (this time the recital begins with a club on the island of Blupblup, the fabled place of origin). But before either a club or a headman's house can be put to use a fire must be lit inside and the smoke ceremonially fanned through the roof. This procedure ensures that the occupants will never be inconvenienced by suffocating fumes. In all villages save Dap a man lights the fire—there the women officiate.

The headman now goes ahead with his interdistrict festival. I shall consider the details at a later date when I discuss the economic system; here it will suffice to say that he orders his men to erect in the center of the village a display platform in the shape of a large overseas canoe. On this platform the villagers place the food—many tons of taro, thousands of coconuts, hundreds of bunches of bananas, and dish upon dish of husked almonds, smoked and ready for eating. At most times the pigs, between twenty and thirty of them, each strapped upside down to a pole, are hung along the sides. The owners paint them with henna stripes and drape them with mats and chains of flowers and fruit.

The guests arrive as appointed, and for at least a day and a night, but sometimes longer, dancing takes place—mimed ballets for the men and more formal movements for the women. At last the division of the food is arranged, and the different families return home with their portions.

Festivals concerned with the headman's nomination of a successor are similar. The father designates the young man by publicly calling on him to carry out ritual, learned specially for the purpose, to enhance the reputation of the village and, incidentally, of himself. The people select two heavy poles to serve as masts (*bwaubwaura*) for the platform, and while they set these up the heir climbs on top and completes the rite. Subsequently, instead of suspending the pigs around the edges of the stage, they lash them one below the other to the masts. The canoe thus acquires a living sail.

This custom is supposed to have been started in Gol, which is built upon rock. With nothing but stone tools digging was difficult, and every time the culture-hero headman of the place, Golaiangaiang, tried to raise masts they fell down. Finally, his mother and one of her cowives in sympathy offered to hold them firm at the base. Their names, Jujuma and Maranika, are still applied to the Gol poles. Golaiangaiang agreed. He excavated two shallow pits, sent the women to the bottom, dropped the poles in, and tied a rope at the other end, which he passed over the ridge of the club. Then he told some of his followers to haul and others simultaneously to push the timbers upright with forked sticks. When the job was half done he walked up to the middle and summoned the birds to cluster round and keep that part steady; and when it was completed he went higher still. Now he hailed the sun. "Hold these masts erect," he urged, "and as they have mounted upward and upward, so pull the name of Gol to the sky till all the heroes of Wogeo and the rest of the islands come to look upon this place as foremost, before all others, famous for its supplies and for its gifts."

The heroes of the other settlements, instead of acquiescing in Gol's assertion of superiority, set out to create ceremonies along the same lines to achieve identical objectives. Today the only differences in the rites are slight changes in the wording of the appeals to the birds and the sun.

Potlatch festivals—an example of fighting with property, in

Codere's phrase[6]—also resemble those connected with a new club, except that usually even greater amounts of food are given away. Inevitably the presence of the *nibek* in a village becomes known everywhere, and the entire island is soon aware of the headman's general intention. But to complete his plan etiquette obliges him to issue the invitation to the feast in his own village in the actual presence of the rival he wishes to humiliate—he cannot do it by messenger. All the leaders therefore keep away, and the victim when finally selected has always to be tricked into making a visit, often by the prospective host feigning a fatal illness. To reverse the position the guest headman must subsequently arrange two festivals, the first to restore the balance, the second to force the earlier aggressor into the position of owing a debt.

On the morning after the festival is finished, when the last visitor has departed, the headman sends the *nibek* back to the world of the spirits. The older men retire to the club, where, occasionally accompanied by the flutes, they sing a series of the songs with which canoe crews keep time when paddling. Meantime those who are younger make for the bush to collect bundles of the coarse-fibered leaves used by carpenters instead of sandpaper. They take these bundles to the club, and old and young alike rub themselves down thoroughly. The underlying idea is that each one will have to serve as a roller over which the *nibek* vessel will be propelled to the shore, and the passage will be rendered easier if their outer surfaces are smooth. When everything is ready the headman entrusts the flutes to the most renowned players for another tune. This tune is the signal for the women to lock themselves away.

The party now descends to the middle of the village and the participants sort themselves out. There are the flautists and sounding-board player, men with torches as yet unlit, some with spears or bows and arrows, and a considerable remainder. All save one of these last, a senior, who remains aloof, form a double line to represent the canoe, and the flutes and the sounding board go to

[6]H. Codere, *Fighting with Property*, Monograph of the American Ethnological Society, No. 38, 1950.

Sending the *nibek* monsters back to the spirit world after an initiation.

the bow and the stern respectively. The torchbearers and those with weapons stand at the side "in the water." Once more the headman asks for music, and as the last note is heard he orders all aboard. The player of the male flute faces seaward with the player of the female immediately behind him. Careful to hold the instruments absolutely horizontal, "to prevent the canoe from capsizing," they place them on the ground on the left-hand side. Now the headman tells the *nibek* to go home. They have eaten the pigs from the village and must wait for another invitation. "Go back, go back, go back," he yells. Immediately the crewmen begin the movements of paddling, and the torchbearers light up and tramp through the settlement accompanied by the spear and arrow men. They chase the monsters and any ghosts present to the shore and there aim the weapons at them. Meantime the elder who has been waiting picks up the flutes in his left hand, places stoppers of leaves in the holes, and runs with them to the club, where he restores them to their usual place. Everyone now turns to the left, picks up two stones in his left hand, passes them round his head with a counterclockwise motion, and throws them away. Next, the headman, after hastily chewing some ginger, passes along the line spraying saliva, "to remove the coldness of the spirits." Each person then takes a dead branch as a broom and makes his way to the beach, sweeping ahead as he proceeds to make doubly sure that every relic of the sacred ceremony is brushed away. They all bathe, and on returning to the shore they first rub their bodies with ginger and later paint themselves with red ochre—further precautions against the dangers of contact with the supernatural and its resulting chill.

IV   Taboo

The *nibek* monsters, or rather the flutes representing their voices, have a further significance. They symbolize masculinity and hence play a vital part in a male cult. But I must postpone describing this function until after a discussion of the views current about ritual pollution.

All Pacific-island societies make a distinction between the things that are purely secular and the things set apart by reason of their supernatural associations—between the things that can be handled freely and the things to be approached with a caution justified by religious belief rather than rational argument. The former category is adequately covered by our word "profane," but for the latter its English opposite, "sacred," is insufficient; some such extra term as "ritually unclean" or "defiled" is required. Often the notions of sacred and ritually unclean are lumped together under the single heading *tabu* or one of its linguistic variants, and only occasionally are separate expressions available. The inhabitants of the north coast of Guadalcanal in the Solomon Islands, for instance, treat a sacrificial shrine and a parturient female with the same kind of discretion and refer to both as being *ambu*, whereas those from northern Malaita, less than 100 miles away, describe the shrine as *ambu* and the parturient woman as *sua*. Ideas of what is or is not ritually unclean also vary. Thus, while these Guadalcanal folk take no notice of menstrual blood and allow a woman during her periods to go about her duties unimpeded, even to the extent of cooking for her family, those from Malaita consider it to be so serious a source of contamination that they insist on her isolating herself in a special hut well away from the settlement.[1]

The Wogeo follow the common pattern, simply differentiating the nonsecular from the secular or profane. They apply the term *rekareka* to those who have been in contact with the sacred and to those who have been in contact with the ritually unclean. This term is not only unrelated to the expression *tabu*, but may also be considered a euphemism. The word is derived from *reka*, "bad," and ordinarily means "poorly," "uncomfortable," "tainted," or "unwholesome."

Persons who are *rekareka* are held to be dangerous to the community and to themselves and are subject to a number of restrictions. They are expected to take care not to touch anyone else's belongings or food that anyone else is likely to eat, and other people in turn have to avoid contact with them. They are even forbidden to feed hunting dogs (though tidbits offered to pigs are thought to do no harm, possibly because these animals, the general scavengers, could scarcely be prevented from picking up scraps). It is said that if a *rekareka* woman inadvertently or on purpose infringes the regulations, although she may become slightly ill, the victim will contract a fatal disease characterized by swelling of the tissues. But carelessness or malice on the part of a *rekareka* man leads to the death of both himself and the victim. In the interests of public safety, therefore, such folk retire from village life. Depending on the circumstances, they seek a retreat in the furthest corner of the dwelling, in the men's club, or in a hut in the bush. Here they are obliged to take the appropriate measures for the protection of themselves and their companions. After a preliminary meal of hot vegetable curry they go through a period of total abstinence. They do not eat,

[1] I. Hogbin, *A Guadalcanal Society* (New York 1964), pp. 72-92; and *Experiments in Civilization* (London 1939), pp. 102-121.

In my book *Transformation Scene* (London 1951), dealing with the New Guinea village of Busama, I described as "profane" what I have here called "ritually unclean" (p. 213). This was misleading. "Profane" is properly applied to the part of life that is unconnected with religion (see J. Goody, "Religion and Ritual," *British Journal of Sociology*, Vol. 12 [1961], p. 155).

do not drink, do not smoke, do not chew betelnut, do not touch
themselves, usually do not speak above a whisper, and take
care to keep their heads covered with a twist of palm spathe.
Then, after an interval, although raw food, meat, fish, and
water are still forbidden, they are allowed cooked vegetables provided they use a bone fork—cassowary bone for a man, flying-
fox bone for a woman—and coconut fluid provided they suck
it through a straw. Smoking is also permitted so long as the
cigarette is placed in a holder, betelnut chewing so long as
somebody puts the nut in their mouth, and touching the skin
if a bone scratcher is employed—again of cassowary or flying
fox according to the person's sex. And there is now no objec-
tion to conversation in a low voice. The penalty for default is
premature old age. The teeth decay, the flesh becomes wrin-
kled, breathing is difficult, and the hair grows white and falls
out.

Persons who are *rekareka* are thought to be chilled, a state
regarded as unpleasant in the extreme. Anyone who is cold feels
heavy and lethargic and hence is unable to withstand the on-
slaught of sorcery. The sick, even when in a fever, are said to be
cold; the effects of magic can be neutralized by dousing the medicines with cold water; and the specialist, before reciting ritual
formulae, always chews ginger to ensure their efficacy. Heat is
essential for living, and without it impotence and loss of vitality
are inevitable. This notion is enshrined in a number of popular
sayings, such as "Warmth of the sun [sometimes phrased
"Warmth of fire"] is mother and father," and "Warmth comes
with full belly."

The Wogeo attitude is apparently the reverse of that of many
African peoples. The New Guinea situation is in fact summed up
accurately by the following quotation, from an account of the
South African Lovedu, in which I have changed the expressions
for hot and cold. "[Warmth] denotes a state of euphoria: man and
matter to be in order and function properly have to be kept
[warm]. . . . On the other hand, [cold], as the antithesis of the
main basis of man's security . . . , is conceived as a destructive
force leading to a state of dysphoria. . . . [Cold] affects the physical

potency of medicines and charms . . . and the welfare of the whole country."[2]

The contrast may be explained by the fact that in Africa, predominantly a hot dry continent, coolness is associated with the life-giving rain bringing relief, whereas the climate of Wogeo is too wet, and the people would say too cold, for comfort. Here, then, the occasional sun appears to foster growth and hence is so welcome. It is noteworthy that all the most important magic to promote a bountiful harvest is aimed at banishing the rain and bringing dry, sunny weather (see below, pp. 175-176).

Approved methods for patients to use to defeat the cold are toasting themselves before blazing fires, applying ginger root or ginger leaves externally in liberal quantities, and consuming hot curry. The method for preparing this dish is to dice unripe bananas and taro and to boil the pieces till tender in a mixture of salt water, fresh water, and the fluid from green coconuts. Grated raw taro is then added as thickening, together with the peppery leaves of the *nies* plant and the pungent fruit of the *weil* plant. The mixture is brought to a boil once more, and before serving the cook stirs in a quantity of coconut cream. Sometimes also the patients, like those who are really ill, have to submit to bleeding "to let out the cold." An operator is summoned and makes an incision with a piece of volcanic glass on their insteps, calves, thighs, buttocks, hands, forearms, arms, and shoulders.

Continual emphasis is placed on the left hand, "because you work with the right"; in other words, there is at such times a reversal of ordinary forms (though the odd individual who is naturally left-handed is not expected to change over). Those who are *rekareka* have to pick up various things with the left hand, or at certain points in a ceremony turn to the left and perhaps stamp with the left foot.

The period of isolation is brought to a close by ritual bathing, and then the person concerned either makes an offer of food to

[2] J. D. and E. J. Krige, "The Lovedu of Transvaal," *African Worlds*, D. Forde, ed. (Oxford 1954), pp. 68-89. Cf. the West African Lodagaa, who maintain that death causes heat (J. Goody, *Death, Property and the Ancestors* [London 1962], pp. 231-234, 255-259, 339).

the neighbors himself (or herself) or else waits while close relatives
of the opposite moiety do so on his behalf. These latter encircle
him first in a procession that travels in an counterclockwise direction, from the right to the left.

Social Relations between Men and Women

The state of *rekareka* is bound up with the relations between
the sexes and the relations between living mortals and the spirits.
I shall deal with them in turn.

The social separateness of men and women in ordinary life is
constantly underlined, and generally when working or at leisure
they remain apart. They carry out different tasks, are called on to
accept different family responsibilities, and have different jural
obligations. Yet, although women exert authority only in the
domestic circle and in the wider political sphere are powerless, at
least overtly, they enjoy a higher status than is customary in New
Guinea.[3] Subordinate to men they may be, but emphatically they
are neither pawns nor slaves. The husband, because he is the
stronger, may beat his spouse, but he does so at his peril. All
she has to do by way of retaliation is to touch his food when
next she menstruates and thereby inflict him with a fatal illness.

It is worth mentioning that although betrothal precedes the
marriage of firstborn sons and firstborn daughters, no father is
likely to succeed in giving a girl to a man whom she dislikes. She
would simply run away. For the younger brothers and sisters
elopement is the approved pattern, and here obviously there must
be mutual attraction. Bride price has no place in either a formal
wedding or the reconciliation of the two sets of relatives after the
elopement.[4] Adultery by both sexes is common, but the husband
is not allowed to punish the wife's lover unless he catches the pair

[3]See M. J. Meggitt, "Male-Female Relationships in the Highlands of New
Guinea," *American Anthropologist*, Vol. 66 (1964), special publication, pp. 204-224;
L. L. Langness, "Sexual Antagonism in the New Guinea Highlands," *Oceania*,
Vol. 37, (1966-1967), pp. 161-177; and M. R. Allen, *Male Cults and Secret Initiations
in Melanesia* (Melbourne 1967).
[4]See I. Hogbin, "Marriage in Wogeo," *Oceania*, Vol. 15 (1944-1945), pp. 324-352;
and "The Father Chooses His Heir," *Oceania*, Vol. 11 (1940-1941), p. 21.

in flagrante.[5] Jealous wives have been known to attempt suicide. After the birth of children neither husband nor wife can initiate divorce.

It would be true to say that the two sexes face one another in more or less balanced opposition. Men often criticize women for undermining the perfection of male solidarity. If irritated they are apt to say with a sigh what a peaceful place Wogeo would be if there were no females. Women talk too much and carry tales, thereby giving rise to ill feeling between kinsmen. "Look, quarreling between brothers is unknown before marriage but after marriage usual; that's because the wives put evil thoughts into their heads," one villager explained. He was both exaggerating the harmony of youths and ignoring the fact that with adulthood the interests of brothers tend at some points to be in conflict.

The women's answer is to make fun of the men's self-importance. At a certain stage in a young girl's coming-of-age celebrations, as we shall see presently, the women adjourn to a mountain top and there mock the initiation rite for pubescent lads, something they are supposed to know nothing about. After an interval the men storm the place with sticks and stones and drive them down, but during that evening, unabashed despite the bruises, they hold a feast of their own and again make references to sacred ceremonies from which they are absolutely excluded. On this occasion the men pay no attention and stolidly go about their business as though not a sound is to be heard.

The separateness is reflected in ritual. The established doctrine is that the members of each sex group would be safe and invulnerable, healthy and prosperous, if only they were to keep to themselves and refrain from mixing with members of the other sex group. Clearly this is a counsel of perfection, impossible of achievement. People point out that small boys would die without their mother, that husband and wife are economically dependent on one another, and, above all, that everyone past the early adult stage is at the mercy of the drive to copulate, an impulse that can be stifled only for brief interludes, and then with difficulty. The

[5] I. Hogbin, "Social Reaction to Crime," *Journal of the Royal Anthropological Institute*, Vol. 68 (1938), pp. 223-262.

result is that the entire population is perpetually weakened, liable
to disease and misadventure—males because of their association
with females, females because of their association with males. The
females, however, are the more fortunate in that they are regularly
freed from contamination by the normal physiological process of
menstruation, when the alien elements flow away of their own
accord. The males, on the other hand, are obliged to take positive
measures to ensure such a periodic disinfection. Therefore, the
elders have the job of taking a boy who is on the brink of puberty
and scarifying his tongue, thus ridding him of influences absorbed
during childhood; and later, after attaining maturity, all men have
to make a practice of gashing the penis to induce profuse bleeding.
This latter operation is known as *sara*, but for a few days the same
word, *baras*, is used for the man as for a woman experiencing a
period. That is to say, females regain their purity by natural menstruation, and men regain theirs by artificial menstruation.

Women past the menopause are not a problem, and there is
never any suggestion that they ought now to imitate the men in
purifying themselves artificially. The explanation offered, illogical
though it sounds, is that continuous purging throughout the years
has been sufficient.

It is to be noted that the actual process of menstruation, male
as well as female, is held to be cleansing. The blood discharged,
however, is polluting, and every precaution must be taken both
by the bleeder and by others to avoid contact with it. Yet the
people are not repelled by blood as such, and if a worker cuts
himself, his companions freely volunteer to wipe the wound and
bind it up.

The technique of male menstruation is as follows. First the man
catches a crayfish or crab and removes one of the claws, which he
keeps wrapped up with ginger until it is required. He also collects
various soothing leaves, including some from a plant whose fruit
has a smooth skin of deep purple color. From dawn onwards on
the day that he has fixed he eats nothing. Then late in the afternoon he goes to a lonely beach, covers his head with a palm spathe,
removes his clothing, and wades out till the water is up to his
knees. He stands there with legs apart and induces an erection
either by thinking about desirable women or by masturbation.

When ready he pushes back the foreskin and hacks at the glans, first on the left side, then on the right. Above all, he must not allow the blood to fall on his fingers or his legs. He waits till the cut has begun to dry and the sea is no longer pink and then walks ashore. After wrapping the penis in leaves, he dresses and goes back to the village, where he enters the club. Here he remains for two or three days. Sexual intercourse is forbidden till the next new moon —the soreness, in any event, may take that long to wear off.

A menstruating woman and a menstruating man are alike *rekareka*. They go into retirement, keep warm, and observe food taboos. The only significant differences are, first, that the woman remains at home, where she is not permitted to use the door when going outside to answer a call of nature, and has to leave and enter through a hole in the floor or the wall; second, that she fasts only after the blood has appeared and the man does so beforehand as well; and, third, that although touching another person or another person's property always brings about his death, a guilty woman does not seriously jeopardize herself, whereas a guilty man suffers the same fate as his victim. The reason is simple—men are socially more important.

A girl at the menarche is called a *baras*, the noun (as distinct from being *baras*, the adjective, like a menstruating adult), and is treated in the opposite manner to an older woman. She is not considered to be "truly" *rekareka*, and instead of being segregated is invited to go around the district weeding the taro gardens to bring the owners a good harvest. The scarification of a boy's tongue is in a sense his menarche, though he is never referred to as a *baras*—it is explained that the blood comes from the wrong place. Yet he is fully *rekareka* and must observe the usual restrictions. The persons who suffer most, as I shall explain below, are the elders who draw the blood. They are *rekareka* for a longer time and still under a taboo after the boy has already returned to the village.

At this point it will be as well to say a word or two about the views current on sexual intercourse. Emphatically, the Wogeo people are not Puritans. They approve of pleasure and see nothing wrong in enjoying themselves. Coitus is neither shameful nor immoral—it is simply dangerous. Public opinion condemns indul-

gence only if the union is adulterous or incestuous.[6] The man
avoids feeling the woman's vagina, and he bathes as soon as possible after leaving her, but solely from considerations of health.
There is a slight risk also in his holding the penis more than is
necessary—it has actually penetrated the woman's body. He
therefore habitually squats to urinate, usually with hands clasped
or on the knees. Correspondingly, the woman avoids feeling the
man's penis during sexual intercourse and also bathes afterwards.
Unlike him, however, she is able to adopt the more convenient
posture of standing to urinate. Sexual pollution is also thought to
be a potential source of failure in secular affairs. Accordingly, a
man embarking on an important job, such as the cultivation of an
extra large taro garden and the preparations for the annual rising
of the palolo worm, or performing sorcery or some other weighty
kind of magic, feels that he would be well advised to keep away
from his wife for a few days beforehand; and a woman about to
engage in dyeing sago-leaf fiber for new garments, the trickiest
task she is called on to undertake, rolls up her husband's sleeping
mat to indicate that he must spend the night in the club. I did not
think to enquire, but this may well be one of the reasons for the
ban on intercourse during pregnancy and while the infant is still
at the breast—birth is dangerous for mother and child, and there
is great risk of the child's succumbing to malaria or other disease
during its first year.

The popular attitude might well be thought to encourage
homosexuality, expecially as this is allegedly common among
neighboring peoples of the mainland. Yet in fact homosexual
relations, apart from mutual masturbation by pairs of youths, are
rare in the village. They are admitted to be prevalent among wage
laborers isolated from their womenfolk in compounds, but are said
to be abandoned on the return home. No criticism is offered, and

---

[6]On one occasion the Dap villagers discovered that an elderly widow, who
appeared to me to be on the verge of seventy, was conducting an intrigue with
a youth no more than eighteen. Far from expressing indignation, they were much
amused. I knew the old lady well enough to ask her why she had not packed the
boy off to seek a girl of his own age. Laughingly she replied with a question—did
I imagine that desire had disappeared with her teeth? Moreover, being now so old,
she had no need to fear male contamination.

people remark that a man should be allowed to follow his sexual fancy.[7]

Men are not called upon to menstruate every month. If they did, the prohibition on sexual intercourse until the next new moon would mean a more or less permanent curb on their impulses and a consequent reduction in the size of families. But it is argued that they ought to be regular and never wait too long. The majority, nevertheless, delay until sickness reminds them of the need to act. When an illness has failed to respond to ordinary magical treatment, then the next diagnosis is the presence of female impurities. For this illness there is but one remedy, an immediate *sara* operation to remove them. Another occasion is when the man is already for a different reason *rekareka*—for example, after he has scarified the tongue of one of the youths. He argues that, since in any case he will be obliged to follow the restrictions and taboos, he may as well seize the opportunity for obtaining the benefits of menstruation.

The salutary effects of penile surgery are said to be immediately observable. The man's body loses its tiredness, his muscles harden, his step quickens, his eyes grow bright, and his skin and hair develop a luster. He therefore feels lighthearted, strong, and confident. This belief provides a means whereby the success of all perilous or doubtful undertakings can be guaranteed. Warriors make sure to menstruate before setting out on a raid, traders before carving an overseas canoe or refurbishing its sails, hunters before weaving a new net for trapping pigs.

Bwaruka

The term *rekareka* is also applied to a woman who has just borne a child. There are the usual general implications except that the restrictions, though no more severe, last longer. The result is that she is segregated not in a corner of the dwelling but in a special hut roughly thrown together in the bush outside the village

[7] I. Hogbin, "Puberty to Marriage: a Study of the Sexual Life of the Natives of Wogeo," *Oceania*, Vol. 16 (1945-1946), pp. 188, 205-206.

boundary. The existence of an alternative expression is hardly unexpected. It is *bwaruka*.

Bwaruka is said to have its origin in the blood of the afterbirth, which contains a nine months' accumulation of male impurities. The husband should not have had intercourse with the woman during the pregnancy, but she will have been cooking his food, and they will often have been in one another's company. Further, part of the responsibility for the child rests with him.[8] Thus it is necessary for her to be set apart for many more days than when she is menstruating.

From the blood itself the word comes to be extended to the mother and to the hut. The theory is that she must manage as best she can alone, without the assistance of a midwife. Usually, however, if there is any danger some old woman comes forward and then undergoes the same taboos.[9] At first the mother fasts, and later she uses the traditional fork, drinking straw, cigarette holder, and scratcher. Relatives and neighbors bring curry for her to eat, but they keep their distance and leave her to pick the dishes up off the floor. Not until the new moon appears is she free to emerge. Then she pulls the hut timbers apart and throws them into the sea.

The infant is not *bwaruka*, only *rekareka*. Accordingly, the grandmothers and aunts are able to nurse it from about the third or fourth day.

Three classes of *rekareka* men are also described as *bwaruka*. In each case, because of certain actions voluntarily performed, those concerned are subject to the customary restrictions for weeks instead of days—as with the young mother, until the following new moon. Like her, too, they are required on this account to withdraw from the village to a *bwaruka* hut in the bush. While there they may perform the *sara* operation on themselves three and even four times. They eventually destroy the shelter and deposit the materials not in the sea but behind the club.

One set of such men consists of those who have scarified the

[8]So close is the association of the father with the embryo that often he suffers from morning sickness during the woman's early pregnancy (I. Hogbin, "A New Guinea Infancy," *Oceania*, Vol. 13 [1942-1943], p. 287).

[9]*Ibid.*, pp. 291–292.

tongue of a youth at his initiation. This procedure frees the boy from the pollution resulting from swallowing his mother's milk and sleeping under the same roof with her. The boy is *rekareka* and under taboos for a few days, but the men who perform the operation are both *rekareka* and *bwaruka*. They will have been most careful not to let a single drop of blood fall on them, yet their task is so onerous—in native eyes probably comparable with that of Hercules when he cleaned the Augean stables—that they must be isolated. Even when they emerge once more the interdiction on sexual intercourse is supposed to be in force for a further nine months. Generally they relax, however, after the appearance of the palolo worm (which rises to the surface of the ocean once annually, in November) or, if this comes first, the beginning of the month named after their particular village.[10]

The people recognize that the other uses of *bwaruka* belong to a different category in that the question of liberation from sexual pollution does not arise. The word has been twisted away from its primary meaning to cover something else, they say; a statement that we may interpret as indicating the notion of metaphorical extension.

I mentioned earlier that at times a *rekareka* individual, like someone who is ill, is obliged to summon an expert to let the cold out of his body by means of incisions on legs, buttocks, arms, and shoulders. The men who are metaphorically *bwaruka* are the first of this kind we have met. The operation is performed towards the end of the period of seclusion.

Before a new clubhouse can be erected, or a grand new residence for a headman, the old building should properly have crumbled into decay and left no trace. This would mean a long wait after it had ceased to be fit for habitation, and the men would have nowhere to entertain visitors, the youths would be obliged to seek sleeping accommodation in other places, and the sacred flutes and masks would have to be stored elsewhere. These inconveniences are avoided if the rotting thatch and timbers can be cleared away to make room for reconstruction. The problem is to find someone

[10]See I. Hogbin and P. Lawrence, *Studies in New Guinea Land Tenure* (Sydney 1967), pp. 54–58. Various of the months are referred to by the names of the different villages—Moon of Bariat, Moon of Dap, and so on.

willing to commit the sacrilege. As a rule an elder with the welfare of the community at heart agrees to do the job. He then faces all the pains of being *bwaruka*.

The remaining instance of metaphorical *bwaruka* is the application of the term to the men who make it possible for a headman to nominate an heir to his title. As I explained, the eldest son of each of his several wives is eligible, and he is free to choose between them. The event takes place at the beginning of a huge feast, when a platform is constructed in the shape of a canoe for the display of the food. The final task is the stepping of the two masts from which the carcasses of the pigs can be hung, one below the other in imitation of the sails. The headman coaches his nominee in a magical spell to ensure high reputation and widespread fame. Then, when the poles that will form the masts are ready for erection, he decorates the lad with boars' tusks, the symbol of the office, and leads him forward. The boy steps on the bases of the poles, one foot on each, and as they are slowly elevated he mounts upwards, reciting the spells as he climbs. He clings to the top, lingers for a few minutes, and slides down. He is now *rekareka*, but the three or four men who raised and afterwards fixed the poles are *bwaruka* as well. They go to a bush hut till the next new moon and abstain from intercourse for several months more.

Manivara

Contact with spirits is no less dangerous than contact with a member of the opposite sex. Such beings are held to be very cold indeed, colder even than the chill arising from male-female pollution. Mourners of both sexes, homicides, and the headmen who call up the village *nibek* monsters from the other world and later send them back again have thus to isolate themselves and carry out special rituals, including bleeding by bodily incisions, before resuming ordinary living. They are *rekareka* and subject to the familiar restrictions, but because of their special status, an additional term, *manivara*, is assigned to them.

It might well be thought that *manivara* would be a more appropriate description for those referred to as metaphorically *bwaruka*. This application the villagers denied. A man must be *bwaruka* if he is isolated in a *bwaruka* hut, they insisted; and, in any case, clubhouse ruins and magical masts have nothing whatever to do with spirits.

The period of mourning varies from a few days to several months, depending on the social status of the deceased. For the entire time the members of the bereaved family and anyone else who may have handled the corpse are expected to stay inside the house during the day and to sleep on the grave at night. They fast to begin with and subsequently take forks, drinking straws, cigarette holders, and scratchers. More emphasis than usual is placed on their great need of heat, however, and daily bathing in the sea is also considered advisable.

The chief hazard the homicide faces is pursuit by the avenging ghost of the murdered man. He takes refuge in the club till the next new moon, keeps to the ordinary *rekareka* regime, rubs himself frequently with ginger, and each evening builds up his ferocity by consuming a potion of which the principal ingredients are the pounded jaw bone of a famous warrior of the past, scrapings of crocodile bone (imported from the New Guinea mainland), and the excrement of a wild boar.

The headman, or at times a deputy, summons the *nibek* monsters formally for the *warabwa* festivals and for the initiation of the lads of the residential cluster. Despite the acknowledgment that the creatures do not exist, he is both *rekareka* and *manivara* and obliged to keep within the club till the next new moon. The flautists impersonating the monsters—and this includes practically all the males of the neighborhood past puberty and below middle age—are not *rekareka* but are expected for the same period to abstain from sexual intercourse.

When the flutes make their appearance on the less significant occasions without a special cerem(ᵇ ᵇ headman does not take any precautions, though those wh(ʳuments have still to keep away from the women.

The Context of Sexual Pollution

The notion that women pollute men is common throughout New Guinea; but the idea of men also polluting women has been reported so far only for the Wogeo and the Arapesh, a mainland group located some distance to the west.[11] As these two peoples are comparatively so close together the situation may be characteristic of the entire region, though unfortunately information about the societies in between is not available.

Douglas argued that the dogma of ritual contamination by females may be expected where males find that their authority can be challenged. To support her hypothesis she contrasted the Walbiri Aborigines of central Australia with the Lele of the Congo and the Mae Enga of the New Guinea highlands.[12]

The Walbiri wander over desert country, and the women are under the control of the men both in theory and in practice. A wife lives at a distance from her father and brothers, who therefore are unable to offer her protection. The husband enforces discipline by ruthless force, even to the extent of punishing her with the weapons normally reserved for fighting. His relatives have no right to interfere, and he is not obliged to pay compensation should his violence result in her death. It is impossible for any woman to play one man off against another, and however much the tribesmen try to seduce the wife of a companion, they are in accord about not allowing sexual desire to give an individual female bargaining power or scope for intrigue. Here beliefs about pollution are absent. Menstrual blood is not dangerous and is treated with indifference.

The Lele are poles apart. They see sex as compounded of enjoyment, desire for fertility, and recognition of danger. A wife has the duty of cleansing her husband after intercourse and then of washing herself before she begins cooking. For this purpose she keeps a pot of water outside the village so that she can bathe in secret. The vessel must be well concealed to prevent the men from accidentally upsetting it and thereby impairing their vigor.

[11]M. Mead, "The Mountain Arapesh," *Anthropological Papers, American Museum of Natural History*, New York, Vol. 36 (1938), pp. 139–349; Vol. 37 (1940), pp. 317–345; and Vol. 40 (1947), pp. 161–419.

[12]M. Douglas, *Purity and Danger* (London 1966), Chapter 9. Material on the Walbiri came from M. J. Meggitt, *Desert People* (Sydney 1962); on the Lele from M. Douglas, *The Lele of the Kasai* (London 1963); and on the Mae Enga from M. J. Meggitt, "Male-Female Relationships in the Highlands of New Guinea," *American Anthropologist*, Vol. 66 (1964), special publication, pp. 204–224.

Should she neglect her ablutions, then anyone who afterwards eats a meal she has prepared becomes impotent. While menstruating she is not only a danger to her husband but also, if she enters a forest, a menace to the community. Hunting becomes difficult, and rituals based on plants that grow wild cease to be effective.

The Lele social system continually founders on female maneuvers undermining male claims for dominance. The men's rivalries are expressed in the struggle for wives. A man without a partner has no status at all, but if he has one he can begin to rise by begetting children and thus qualifying for entry into the various cult associations. With a daughter he can demand the services of a son-in-law, and with several, especially if there are also granddaughters, he is high up on the ladder of privilege. This ascendency occurs because he can use the girls to build up a following of affines. The fact that polygyny is permitted means that the competition for women is intense. From a man's point of view, therefore, females are the most desirable objects the society can offer.

A Lele girl grows up a coquette, the center of affectionate and flirtatious attention. Her husband never gains more than limited control over her. True, he has the right to beat her, but if he then loses her affection she is free to dismiss him. Other suitors clamor for her, and she can pick whom she likes, carrying on endless intrigues and playing one man off against another. When mother and daughter connive they can easily wreck any plan of which they disapprove. Therefore, ultimately men are obliged to assert their vaunted superiority by charming, coaxing, flattering, and wheedling.

Mae Enga men have still more difficulties to face. From adolescence onwards males are taught to shun the company of the opposite sex, and they go into periodical seclusion to purify themselves from chance contacts. Only a husband can risk sexual intercourse because the remedies for protecting virility are available solely to those who are married. But even in wedlock men fear coitus and reduce the occasions to the minimum necessary for procreation. Above all, they are terrified of menstrual blood.

Enga organization is based on exogamous patrilineal clans, which are compact political units, each one the enemy of all the

rest. Wives therefore necessarily come from hostile groups. A
man strives fiercely for prestige by exchanging pigs and valuables
with partners who also belong to clans that are at odds with his
own. So each person is in ceremonial and military rivalry with his
affines. The equation of femininity with peril is explained by the
fact that the marriage relationship has to bear such a multiplicity
of strains and tensions.

Douglas backed up her case with further evidence from the
Nuer of the Sudan and the Nambudiri Brahmins of Malabar (no
pollution), and the Yurok of California and the Bemba of Rhodesia
(pollution). The basic problem, she said, "is a case of wanting to
have your cake and eat it." The Lele man wants to use women as
pawns and yet will take sides with individual females against other
males; the Mae Enga man wants to fight enemy clans and yet
marry their womenfolk; and the Bemba woman wants to be free
and independent and to behave in ways that will inevitably
threaten to wreck her marriage and yet to retain her husband. "In
each case the dangerous situation which has to be handled with
washings and avoidances has in common with the others that the
norms of behaviour are contradictory. The left hand is fighting the
right hand . . . Is there any reason why these examples of the social
system at war with itself are drawn from sexual relations? . . . The
answer may be that no other social pressures are potentially so
explosive as those which constrain sexual relations. We can come
to sympathize with St. Paul's extraordinary demand that in the
new Christian society there should be neither male nor female." [13]

Is there a clue here to the understanding of Wogeo? I think so.
I said earlier that the Wogeo sexual groups are in balanced opposition. Balanced they are in the sense of being mutually dependent
and of nearly equal status, with men having only a slight edge.
And they are also in opposition. Men continue to claim authority
and to feel that they have the right to be high-handed; and they
think that their spouses ought to be faithful. But they also know
that troubles tend to arise if they become too domineering, and
that few wives, if any, refrain from taking an occasional lover. As
for the women themselves, they maintain that their wishes should

[13] *Op. cit.*, p. 157

be respected on account of their importance in the economy and the vital part they play in the social system. But they have to smother their resentments at male pretensions and keep their aggressive impulses concealed, for direct and open retaliation for unfair treatment presents difficulties. They can indulge in adulterous intrigues, but it would be unwise for them to flaunt the liaisons in public. Pollution theories provide a solution. These theories give strong men proof that women are inherently inferior and weak women a means of inflicting punishment on men.

It might be thought that a further factor in the situation is the existence of matrilineal groups in a world that is man-made. I do not think so. The moieties regulate marriage and ceremonial but have little or nothing to do with the daily routine. Further, succession always, and inheritance generally, follow the male line. A father allots land to his daughter only if his sons will not suffer thereby.

V   Initiation

The fact that the *nibek* flutes symbolize masculinity is clearly brought out in the myth of their origin. A culture heroine of Maluk village became ill during pregnancy and died. Her parents buried the body under the house, as was the custom. The embryo in her womb did not perish, however, and when born it kept itself alive underground by sucking the sticky white sap from the roots of a breadfruit tree standing close by. The child grew and grew, and one day the old couple heard it crying. They at once exhumed it and recognized the little boy it had now become as a grandson, whom they decided to call Nat Karamwang (literally "man locust").

Some time later, when Nat Karamwang had reached adolescence, two heroines, Malaun and Sinamo, from the neighboring island of Koil, dreamed the notion of making flutes (all inspiration is supposed to come in this way during sleep). They selected two bamboos, cut them to size, and bored a hole near the end. At once both instruments began piping of their own accord—something like a music box. Overjoyed, the women took a drum and danced till they became exhausted. Then they stoppered the hole and went off to the gardens. Nat Karamwang heard the sound all the way across the water and, boylike, was curious. He paddled over in his canoe, found one of the flutes, removed the stopper, and blew into the hole. The noise disturbed the women, who came back to investigate. They started to explain that there was no need for the mouth to be near the hole, but Nat Karamwang, too excited to pay attention, kicked them out of the way. "Very well, Nat Karamwang, you think you know everything!" they shouted in anger. "But perhaps this will surprise you. Because you've stolen for yourself something we'd intended for everybody, no female will from now on look at a flute or have anything to do with one. You males can keep them. And listen! Flutes won't sing by themselves again—you decided to blow this one, and that's the way it shall be. We say to you also that learning what to do won't be easy—no, you'll have to work hard and sweat. A last warning —and this is the truth. If lads of your size don't make the effort to blow properly they'll never never never grow up to be men."

Malaun and Sinamo then set off in disgust for the New Guinea mainland, where for a period they remained. They always declined to go back to Koil or, with scorn, to visit Wogeo, the home of Nat Karamwang; but eventually each did return to the Schouten group, one to Kadovar, the other to Blupblup. Nowadays suitable bamboo for flutes grows therefore only in the three places, the mainland and these two islands. The Wogeo people assert that when a suitable clump has been found the canes are always cut so that, "out of respect," they fall in the direction of the village where the earliest flutes were invented.

I did not see anyone doing so, but it is also said that in memory of Nat Karamwang some men like to eat a roasted locust before a recital. Breadfruit, which saved him in infancy, has a special place in the ritual, as we shall see presently.

The underlying theme of the male cult is again the gulf, physical and social, between men and women. The people sum up the situation in the saying, "Men play flutes, women bear infants." Although a few individuals never really master the art of the flute, the threat in the myth that learning what to do would prove difficult need hardly be taken literally. What is onerous is not so much acquiring a technique as attaining the eligibility to practice it. Each male must pass through a series of initiation ceremonies that begin in babyhood and end in later youth. (Physical handicaps are no bar, though mental deficiency disqualifies.) During the first rite the elders pierce the child's ears; in the second they admit him to the clubhouse, demonstrate the flutes, and present him with clothing; and in the third they scarify his tongue. Not till the wounds are healed is he considered fit to have a lesson in how to play the instruments. Some years afterwards, instruction about incising the penis is given, and finally, at the age of about nineteen, the young man is free to adopt the distinctive headdress of an adult, a wickerwork cone through which the hair is drawn.

In theory the ceremonies are correlated with growth, and the boy gains entry not only to a sex group, the central consideration, but also to successive age grades with ever increasing obligations.[1] Thus the ears should be pierced at the end of infancy, at about three; admission to the club granted in midchildhood, at about nine; and the tongue scarified at puberty. But all sorts of factors may prevent the attainment of the ideal. Many of the performances demand the outlay of wealth, and their organization has in consequence to be left to a headman or an elder of nearly equal status. Ordinary folk then take advantage of the opportunity and introduce their sons, who may be older or younger than is considered proper. At one ceremony I attended the lads' ages varied by as much as five years. Also, pressure from an aged relative, conscious of his failing health, may force the father's hand. Marigum found himself obliged to have his son Dal taught the ritual of penis incision about three years too early. The boy's maternal grandfather, who loved him dearly and considered him almost a projection of his own personality—they were namesakes—kept on insisting. The old man did in fact die shortly afterwards.

The initiation cycles of African tribes are often referred to in the literature as "schools," and the accounts record that the boys' guardians accompany religious tuition with systematic training in secular matters, such as the various social requirements (respect for the aged and the nobility, consideration for women, duties to kinsfolk, and so forth), the history and traditions of the commu-

---

[1]The following is a list of the terms for persons of different sex and age: *ramat* = a human being, person; *moana* = a male; *veini* = a female; *nat* = a male between puberty and maturity; *natnat* = a male who has not yet learned to incise the penis; *marita nat* = a male child; *moana bitang* = a mature man with a family (*bitang* = big); *nat yata-ata* = a tall male, an older youth, a young man; *nat samagun* = a naked male, a boy not yet clothed; *yamun* = an initiand; *veini wama* = a woman with a family; *kirigirig* = a female child; *inabwe kirigirig* = an older girl who has not yet menstruated; *baras* = a girl who is menstruating for the first time, an unmarried girl, menstruating (of a woman or a man).

nity, hunting lore, and even astronomy. As a rule, the African seniors also administer endurance tests. They may supply their charges with inaccurate information for catching game and later warn them to be silent when beaten for incompetence; or they may pelt them with flaming branches and then punish them for allowing themselves to be burned.

Wogeo is different. The purpose of the rites here is to make certain that the boy will grow into a man, and the elders direct all their endeavours to this end. They proceed step by step: In his infancy they pierce his ears, convinced that only by such means can he attain childhood; in his childhood they take him from his mother and insist on his sleeping at night in the clubhouse, basing their action on the belief that if he were to remain with her he would never reach puberty; in his pubescent period they scarify his tongue to enable him to play the flutes, thinking that only by so doing can he arrive at youth; and in his youth they show him how to incise the penis on the understanding that without menstruating he cannot advance to manhood. Everything else is incidental. Myths, if referred to at all—and to my certain knowledge at one set of ceremonies they were not—are narrated haphazardly, even in perfunctory fashion, as bystanders happen to remember them. Occasionally they give advice—they may tell the boy that he is now too big to cry, or old enough to perform some task, or sufficiently aware to understand a complicated piece of information—but there is no predetermined formal exhortation as part of a routine. True, the initiand is called upon to submit to unpleasant ordeals; scraping the tongue and cutting the penis, for example, cause much pain. He is also slapped around the shoulders, stretched, forced to chew acrid roots, forbidden to swallow, and made to fast. But at such times tears, screams, grumbles, and complaints do not give rise to criticism or chiding; indeed, the seniors may show sympathy. They regret the unpleasantness and offer as explanation the urgent necessity of fulfilling the demands of ritual lest a worst fate should befall. The idea of cultivating hardihood does not seem to occur to them.

I shall give the details of what happens, beginning with the earliest ceremony.

Ear Piercing

Every child must have his ear lobes pierced, but the rite itself is not held to be as grave as the others. So in villages where the headmen are unwilling to take over the organization, perhaps because the last of their male offspring has already undergone the operation, fathers do not feel disgraced if a son has to wait until the older lads are seeing the flutes for the first time, or are having their tongues scarified, or until the boy can be sent to a neighboring settlement where relatives are arranging to hãve the ears of their children attended to.

During my stay, only one ear-piercing ceremony took place. This ceremony was in Maluk, and I attended with my fellow villagers from Dap. The son of the headman Mwanubwa had been weaned for some time and was beginning to speak with reasonable fluency. Accordingly, the father approached a Bwanag headman to whom he was closely related, a man of the opposite moiety to the child. This person agreed to perform the ceremony and fixed the date. The news spread quickly, and other related headmen, from Dap and Job, announced their intention of being present. Two other Maluk householders also spoke up and said they would like their sons to be included. This pair made their own arrangements for the attendance of operators. Each sought out a kinsman of his choice, one a maternal uncle from Gol, the other a Maluk cross cousin. There was no necessity for picking anybody of a particular kinship status, they told me. He ought to be from the opposite moiety, but this requirement could on occasion be waived.

The people from Bwanag, Dap, and Job reached Maluk on the afternoon of the day previous to that named. There were four or five men from each place, including the headmen, all of whom had brought along a pair of flutes in honor of the host. Numbers of women also came bearing baskets of food as a gift from the husband.

That night we went to bed early to be ready for arising before dawn to call up the monsters. Later, after breakfast of curry in the clubhouse, most of the visitors adjourned to a secluded area to perform on the flutes. Meanwhile the village folk collected the food supplies. Mwanubwa furnished two pigs, his brother one, the other Maluk headman one, and the fathers of the extra boys one each. The animals were brought trussed up, with the legs fastened to a pole, and decorated with stripes of red ochre, strings of fruit, and coconut-leaf streamers. The men carried them to the front of the club; the youths brought coconuts, areca nuts, and betel pepper; and the women piled ropes of bananas and baskets of taro and nuts alongside.

At about four in the afternoon, on a signal from Mwanubwa, the visitors came back to the village with the flutes. At once the women seized the children and went indoors. The younger men now formed into two parties, one before the club entrance, the other at a distance of fifty yards. There was no principle of division, and each individual chose for himself. Thus locals and visitors were to be found in both. Suddenly one of the elders struck a sounding board ("the *nibek's* bone"), and they rushed at each other with fists flying. They were without weapons, but one man grabbed a dog that was wandering down the street and slung it at the face of an opponent. A youth killed the frightened animal, and the carcass went on the pile of food, to be roasted with the pigs. The fracas continued for about five minutes, when the headmen and other elders present called loudly for order.

This was a ritual fight during which the rules of correct behavior were suspended. Normally a man of one moiety does not strike a member of the other, no matter how enraged he may be; now, for the short interval, he can harm him as much as he likes —blacken his eyes even—always provided he does not resort to weapons. Similarly, brother may strike brother, brother-in-law punch brother-in-law. My friends explained how the need for daily cooperation ensures that ordinarily people will live together in peace. But this does not mean an absence of resentment; the bitterness is there, but expediency ensures that it is pushed below the surface. Every so often, on occasions such as this, an emotional purging takes place. People give vent to their hidden feelings and thereby expel them. Then a fresh start can be made. One man reminded me of the oft-quoted proverb, "If you're angry with your wife, smash a pot; otherwise you'll be angry for a month." Vexation bottled up for too long might lead to murder, added another, and periodic expression of it is therefore salutary. Cuts and bruises notwithstanding, probably they were right. It appeared that harmony was reestablished and that those who a few seconds before had been belaboring one another were once more ready to laugh and joke together. There is also the argument that a formal reversal of the norms for a brief period has the effect of bringing home to everybody what the ideal is.

Each of the men who had consented to operate now entered the house where the patients and their mothers were hiding. They grasped the boys by the shoulders, blindfolded them with bandages of bark cloth, and pushed them outside. The flutes remained silent, but against a background of the crashing noise of sounding boards they thrust a sliver of bone from a flying fox through the lobe and top of each ear of the initiands, all three of whom were yelling loudly from fright. After forcing coils of Cordyline leaf into the holes, they rubbed the small bodies all over with crushed ginger plant. "There, the *nibek* monsters have bitten you; they've made their first mark and will come back later when they're ready and eat you up," they said. "Now go back to your mother and ask for some curry. Away with you; off you go."

The youths present now carried the pigs and other food to the beach, where they lit fires and went ahead with the cooking. The visitors ate a meal with pork then and there, but the bulk of the supplies they carried home the next day, after the monsters had been dispatched across the sea. Back in their own villages they shared the portions with the other men. The meats of initiation would be fatal to women, and they received nothing.

Admission to the Club

As well as entry into the club, the events of the next stage are the demonstration of the flutes and the adoption of clothing. The club, however, is of chief importance. In midchildhood a boy must be removed as far as is feasible from his mother and the female influences she exudes; these influences would sap his strength and stunt his growth. It is agreed that in many respects he will continue to be dependent upon her, but already he should be learning about what, in the social sense, being male means. With this end in view, the elders see that he goes to the club and henceforth sleeps there. The harmful effect of ashes on the skin of a growing lad is a further reason for concern. Dogs are the main danger. When in search of food they are apt to scratch at the embers of a dead cooking fire, scattering dust on the bed mats nearby. The club is a haven from the danger; high off the ground, it is reached by means of a ladder or a notched log that an animal cannot easily climb.

In places where the club is in ruins awaiting renewal the initiands go to a room set aside in the apsidal end of one of the dwellings or to a village not far away.

If the boys are to have the freedom of the club, they will necessarily see the flutes and other sacred paraphernalia kept there. The surrounding ritual of the initiation ceremony is to impress upon them that they now belong to a new world and share secrets never disclosed to the other sex. And if they are to be at one with men, it is fitting also that they should be invested with the most essential of the men's garments, the corselet of bark. Some people assert that this has the added advantage of protecting the navel, still vulnerable to pollution, and compressing the abdomen to produce the slim upright figure considered desirable (young children, because of the enormous amounts of carbohydrates consumed, are always pot-bellied).

Marigum's youngest son, Sabwakai, had been admitted to the Dap club shortly before I landed, and the details were fresh in the people's minds. Then, not long before I departed, a similar ceremony took place in Gol, and I was able to confirm the reports by direct observation.

Sabwakai was about ten years of age. He had had five Wonevaro companions, two a little older, three a little younger. One came from Mwarok, one from Kinaba, two from Job, and one from Bariat. Eleven pigs were provided, one each by the boys' fathers, one each by Sabwakai's maternal grandfather and maternal uncle, and one each, as a compliment to Marigum, by the other Dap headman, a headman of Kinaba, and a headman of Falala. In Gol there were five boys, also of varying ages, the youngest the son of a headman, the remainder from various families in the same village. This time there were nine pigs, one each from the officiating headman and his brother-in-law (the son's maternal uncle), the other boys' fathers, and headmen of Dap, Kwablik, and Ga.

Preparations occupied the first day. The local men and youths caught their pigs, tied them up, and collected the usual decorations. They and the women also brought in loads of food, including taro, coconuts, bananas, and almonds; and they saw to it that there were stocks of firewood, areca nuts, betel pepper, and tobacco. During the afternoon the visitors arrived bearing the rest of the pigs and extra vegetables.

The boys were aware of what was afoot, and that evening the mothers cooked them a heavy meal, the last that they would eat for several days. One dish was of the nuts called locally *wasek* (*Terminalia kaerndachii*), reserved primarily for export to the mainland. Women and young people may eat them but not initiated men. Here then was a symbolic farewell to childhood.

The father had already chosen the man to take his son into the club. This sponsor or guardian, as was mentioned, ought always to be of the opposite moiety to the boy's; but nobody seemed to object very strongly if the two belonged to the same unit.

As usual, the *nibek* monsters were summoned before dawn, but for the time being the flutes remained on the beach in the care of a few older men instead of being carried to the village.

After daylight the sponsors entered the club, and, while the rest of the villagers looked on, the different parents (or foster parents if the true parents were dead) daubed their child with red ochre and led him by the hand to the bottom of the ladder at the entrance. The sponsors descended one by one, pushed the mother away, gave the boy a smart slap on the shoulders with the open palm to expel some of her influence at once, took him from his father, and bore him up the steps. Several of the lads were so terrified that they made a mess of themselves, and in Dap this part of the ceremony was delayed for over an hour while one of them who had run away was recaptured from high up in the branches of a tree. The sponsors lifted their charges to a broad shelf under the thatch and tried to sooth their fears with the assurance that if they lay still and made no noise the swallowing by the monsters would not be painful. The mothers ran weeping to the houses, where they sang mournful airs while cooking dishes of curry.

The ritual fight followed. Ostensibly one party represented the insistent community, the other the unwilling parents; but as before each person chose a group to suit himself. At Gol excitement ran so high that the contest began too soon, before the signal on the sounding board, and the combatants surged up and down the ladder and in and out of the club. I was caught in a corner and when peace was restored found my shirt and trousers drenched with blood—other people's, not my own. The paternal and maternal uncles endeavored to placate both sides by clubbing dogs and offering them as additional fare for the feasts. In Gol no less than seven carcasses appeared. The women cried even more loudly than before when they saw their pets dispatched.

As soon as the wounds had been patched up, the youths carried the pigs and other supplies to the beach, where the men with the flutes were quietly waiting. The host headman detailed half a dozen of his more active followers to be the cooks for the entire period of the celebrations. This work put them under a taboo; they were subject to various minor restrictions and, above all, were not allowed to touch the initiands. They at once prepared enough for a hearty meal for all present. The remainder of the meat they baked lightly, enough to prevent its going bad. The afternoon passed in flute playing and jocularity. As usual, the women kept their distance and received not so much as a crumb.

Meantime the boys sat or slept in the club. The mothers provided them with curry, but the guardians warned them to eat sparingly. They told them also that when going outside to answer a call of nature they must not walk more than a few paces or lift their eyes from the ground. At the same time, they did their best to be reassuring by minimizing the severity of the trials ahead. They said that a lad who heeded all the warnings need have no worries.

At dusk the men on the beach came back, again leaving the flutes. Most of them spent the night in the club, where they sang and played hand drums. The internal dimensions of the Gol building were twenty feet by twelve, and there were two fires burning. The number of occupants never fell below sixty, exclusive of the boys on the shelf above. At intervals different women approached and handed up a platter of curry, which all ate with relish. The smoke was suffocating and the stench of sweaty bodies abominable, but everyone enjoyed himself.

In the morning several of the younger men slipped out before the rest were fully awake. They spent some time in making themselves hideous with streaks and circles of pipeclay and charcoal and then returned, whooping at the tops of their voices. They seized the boys by the shoulders and ankles, pulling and stretching as they did so, and carried them down to the beach. The guardians followed and took charge. They pointed to the flutes, demonstrated how these were played, and explained that here were the monsters. This was all that "being swallowed" meant. Then each led his ward into the sea. He pulled on the boy's ankles and wrists to make him grow quickly and scrubbed him hard all over with sand and salt water to remove every trace of the gastric juices and excrement left from the monsters' bowels. Then he called to a relative waiting, spear in hand, on the shore. This man advanced into the water, twisted the blade of his weapon in the boy's hair, and by this means hauled him ashore. The procedure had the magical intention of stretching him and so promoting his growth. The guardians now shepherded their charges back to the club, leaving the others for a morning of music and eating.

Once the lads were safely reinstalled, the men offered them a full explanation of what had taken place. There were no supernatural beings, only flutes, they said. These were the mysteries that must be hidden from the women. In a few years the boys would be taught how to play the tunes. The entire affair had been invented long ago by the culture heroes to turn children into men —to separate them from their mothers, to make them grow, and to prepare them for handling the instruments. For these reasons the people of today carry on the tradition. In each successive generation fathers have initiated the sons who would follow them. But the women must never learn the truth—if they did, they might laugh and poke fun. It was at this point that one of the Gol guardians related a myth as a fearful example. Wopa, from Kinaba, was a growing youth who had just completed his initiation, he began. One morning, after the adults had departed for the cultivations, this lad gathered the children of both sexes together and

taught them how to perform a mock initiation ceremony. He stole
the flutes from the club, cut the boys' and the girls' tongues, and
showed them how to blow. The fathers, on learning what had
taken place, were appalled. They bashed out the boys' brains with
bludgeons, cut the girls' throats, and buried the bodies in the bush.
Wopa alone escaped. First he ran to the mountains and hid in a
cave, which may still be seen. But the men pursued him, and he
was obliged to crawl back under cover of darkness to the beach.
Here he took a canoe and sailed for the New Guinea mainland.
Realizing that he would never again be accepted at home, he
taught the people of the village where he landed as much about
the rites as he could remember. His memory was faulty, and to
this day the performances of the mainland communities remain
a botched jumble.

Around noon the men and youths brought the flutes to the
club, and for a while the playing went on there. The principal task
of the rest of the day was the adorning of the initiands. For this
purpose they were taken below, where the light was better. The
closer relatives from both sides—the paternal and maternal uncles,
the older brothers, and the cousins—brought bundles of dyed
rattan imported from the mainland and proceeded to weave multicolored bands around their wrists, upper arms, ankles, waists,
and necks. The job is extremely delicate and tedious, and only
those with good eyesight are able to carry it out—obviously all of
them are under the age of about forty-five. They retain the many
different patterns in their heads, and each worker has his favorites.
A needle of palm midrib about eight inches long is used, with a
point at one end and an eye for the cane cut into the other. Soft
leaves are wrapped around the boys first to protect the skin from
being pricked and to prevent the band from becoming too tight.
These leaves are pulled out later.

At nightfall the cooks prepared another meal, though the boys
continued to eat nothing but curry. In the morning the rattan
bands were completed, and each boy received clothing from his
senior maternal uncle. Next the guardian rubbed him with a
mixture of coconut oil and ochre till his skin shone like burnished
copper; and finally the father, uncles, and other kinsfolk hung
necklaces and shell bands upon him and stuck bird-of-paradise

plumes and cockatoo feathers in his hair. All was now ready for
the descent and ceremonial procession around the village. First,
led by the guardian, came the son of the man who had arranged
the rites, next a couple of his slightly older brothers or cousins as
support; then guardian and a lad of the opposite moiety and a few
of his relatives; then guardian and a lad of the same moiety as the
leader; and so on. Marching in single file in a clockwise direction
(that is, turning to the right), they encircled the central space
between the houses while bystanders beat time on hand drums.
The women looked on, many of them moved to tears at the
thought of the boys' escape from the entrails of the monsters, but
even the mothers made no move to embrace their offspring. Eventually sponsors and initiands returned to the club, and again the
women brought bowls of curry. The men adjourned to the beach
to finish the remnants of the pork. Later the majority of the
visitors said farewell and left for home.

The boys spent the next few days strolling around in their
finery and paying calls on other settlements even though as yet
only curry was allowed. While they were at this activity the
residents of their own village regularly went fishing and in the
evening smoked the catch. The preserved fish and a pig from one

Parade of the young initiands in Gol village.

of the headmen provided the basis of a small feast. The guardians stood the boys in a line outside the club, and several youths stepped forward bearing the food in wooden dishes. They encircled the lads three times, traveling on this occasion in counterclockwise direction, to the left. The biggest portion went to the headman's house, where the boys had their first proper meal, but each of the households received at least one dish.

After the meal the monsters could be sent away. The headman also performed a rite of purification over the cooks, who subsequently went off to incise the penis. They returned to their ordinary duties a few days later, but avoided their wives for the rest of the month.

One last ceremony remained. At various spots in the foothills below the central peaks streams emerge from limestone caverns and descend in a series of pools separated by falls or cascades. An older youth, at Gol the elder brother of one of the lads, assembled all the boys and conducted them to the nearest of the brooks, where he bade them drink of the cleansing waters of the topmost basin. They arranged themselves in pairs, one partner from each moiety, so that both could immerse their faces simultaneously. The two were now considered to be blood brothers (*wasabwai*), closer than siblings.[2] They could refuse one another nothing and were mutually useful later in arranging assignations.

Before passing on, I should say a word or two about the boys' subsequent attitude toward the *nibek* monsters. It might be thought that they would be sadly disappointed and probably contemptuous of the elders for hoodwinking them with a silly fraud. This is not so. I frequently heard adolescents laughing among themselves at their earlier anxiety about what they had thought might happen to them; but they never gave the impression of thinking they had been imposed upon or let down, and they were

[2]Similar relationships have been recorded from many parts of the Pacific. As the pair are already related before the ceremony of union takes place, the term "blood brotherhood" seems preferable to that of "bond friendship," which I used in an earlier publication. (At the same time, it must be admitted that there is no notion of the blood coagulating as a penalty for default.) Today the pidgin-English expressions *foroman* and *wanein* (literally "one name") have practically ousted *wasabwai*. See I. Hogbin, ":Puberty to Marriage: A Study of the Sexual Life of the Natives of Wogeo," *Oceania,* Vol. 16 (1945–1946), pp. 191-194.

not angry. Clearly they were convinced that anything appertaining to the flutes must be taken very seriously indeed—the restrictions observed and the taboos honored. If hoax there was, then it was directed less at the young males than at the female half of the population.

Scarifying the Tongue

I have spoken of the belief that a boy cannot become a man unless he performs on the flute. It is also thought that there would be no hope of his taking in the rudiments of the art without the prior elimination of the injurious elements absorbed from females during his infancy and childhood. Tongue scarification is thus a necessary prelude to his earliest lessons. It is in a sense his first artificial menstruation, corresponding with the initial natural menstruation of a pubescent girl. The tongue is selected for the bleeding because hitherto he will have absorbed the worst of the pollution orally with mothers' milk; moreover, cleansing the tongue renders it pliable and hence better fitted for coping with a woodwind instrument. In a few years, when he is sufficiently mature for sexual intercourse, the penis will be the agent whereby the contamination is transferred. Accordingly, in later life this is the organ that receives menstrual treatment. The advantage, in religious terms, is that it too is now better fitted for coping with the tasks expected of it.

No tongue scarification took place while I was on the island, and my account is necessarily based on hearsay.

The operation is a more serious matter than the entry into the clubhouse, and a ritual specialist is required for it. He holds the title of "headman of the beach," but acts as a leader solely on this occasion. In every residential cluster there is at least one such specialist, frequently a younger brother or half-brother of the proper headman. The essential qualification for office is inheritance from the father or a paternal uncle of secret knowledge of the rituals and magic.

The specialist and his assistants are said to be *bwaruka* after the operation, but are subject to even heavier restrictions than is usual for people in this condition. Thus, in addition to having to observe dietary and other taboos they are forced to refrain from ordinary undertakings not for one month only but for several. Similarly, although the boys are referred to as "just *rekareka*," they too are not allowed to resume village life at the end of a mere couple of days. Further, in commemoration of the infancy of Nat Karamwang, the food most favored for them is breadfruit. In practice, scarification takes place solely when breadfruit is plentiful. Breadfruit trees are never completely bare, but there is a real harvest season. People say, however, that this season varies from year to year and cannot be forecast more than a couple of months ahead (in 1934 the main crop ripened in late May and June). Should supplies give out before the end of the seclusion period the specialist is prepared to sanction bananas as a substitute—but these must be stolen from distant villages and so not cultivated by anyone directly concerned in the initiation. It is, of course, common throughout the world for those in a transitional state, such as initiands, to be exempt from observing the regular rules of conduct.

It will be convenient to list the other taboos on the boys before I proceed to describe the rites in chronological order: On the first day they must sit with the mouth open and tongue out. They are forbidden to swallow even saliva and may not eat, drink, or speak. On the second day they may not handle food, fluid containers, or their own or anyone else's skin; but they may eat the minute portions of pounded raw breadfruit that the assistants place in their mouths and drink coconut fluid through a straw held for them. On the third day handling food, fluid containers, and the skin are still forbidden; but they may eat a little cooked breadfruit on the end of a fork and hold the straw themselves to suck up coconut fluid. They may not speak aloud.

Scarification follows puberty, when the boy "has acquired a little understanding and can be trusted not to swallow the blood from his tongue"—also, though this fact is less often stressed, when his services are beginning to be an economic asset to the household. As the normal sort of feasting is out of the question and supplies do not have to be accumulated, the operation could be performed during the next breadfruit harvest following on the growth of his pubic and axillary hair. But this time the elders give thought to the discomforts of those of their number who will have to share the taboos. As a rule they procrastinate until several youths can be put through together. Some of these may have been waiting for three or four years. The specialist has the sole right to fix the date but is generally amenable to the arguments of impatient fathers, even of impatient sons.

His first task is to enlist the help of three or four assistants, who will also act as guardians. They may be of either moiety but should not be closely related to their charges lest their sympathy become too deeply engaged and disturb their peace of mind. Paternal and maternal uncles, for instance, are alike barred. The most usual volunteers are householders of some maturity. The younger men have family responsibilities and cannot neglect everyday tasks; and the aged, already failing, do not care to risk their health further.

The specialist has the assistants direct the boys in the construction of a hut in which they will all live during the forthcoming weeks. He picks a site in a clearing close to the shore but with big trees growing nearby to give protection from the wind.

A fine day is essential, and as soon as the prospects are fair the specialist asks the assistants to tell the boys' relatives—the father, uncles, elder brothers, and older cousins—to bring down quantities of breadfruit and green coconuts. They bring the food and withdraw, though some of them may remain sitting at a comfortable distance. The assistants collect on their own account certain roots with an acrid taste and also leaves well known for their soft spongy texture. The specialist himself gathers ginger, a bundle of the coarse leaves used by carpenters in place of sandpaper, and a handful of crimson Cordyline leaves. Every specialist has his own spells for the different substances, and these he now recites. The Dap formula for the sandpaper leaves runs:

> "The pollution flows away with the blood.
> Come, southeast trade wind, enter the boys' tongues,
> Give them your breath to blow the flutes.
> Come, northwest monsoon, enter the boys' tongues,
> Give them your breath to blow the flutes.
> Come south wind, east wind, northerly breeze, westerly
> breeze,

Come all tempests and hurricanes from everywhere,
Enter the boys' tongues,
Give them your breath to blow the flutes."

The recital ends with a whistling noise in imitation of the sound
of the flutes. The Gol formula is similar, not identical, and also
mentions the name of a local culture hero, Nat Egare (literally
"orphan"), who had no relatives. He initiated himself to such good
effect that if he played a flute shorter than man's height the sound
was so loud that the bamboo immediately shattered in pieces. In
Bariat the corresponding spell enumerates various birds that have
a recognizable call.

When all is ready the specialist kindles several fires in a row,
again accompanying the work with magic. He is careful to see
that these fires have absolute protection from the breeze so that
the smoke will rise vertically to the top of the trees. To each boy
he assigns one fire in particular. He passes down the front with
orders for them to open the mouth, and, "to make them warm,"
he spits chewed ginger inside. They then have to bite well into
the acrid roots that he holds in his hands "for the tongue to tingle,
swollen with all the blood." The assistants now make sure that
every boy has his legs wide apart, head bent forward over the
flames, and tongue thrust out. The specialist walks down the back
of the line, pausing to give each lad's tongue a scrape with the
sandpaper leaves. He attends to the tongue first on the left side,
then on the right, then on the upper surface. He tries to be gentle
but is not satisfied till the blood is falling steadily drop by drop.
Contact with it is death, and the assistants continually warn him
to watch his hands and the boys to guard their legs from splashes.
"Legs right out of the way, heads on top of the fire, tongue out
as far as you can manage, and, remember, don't swallow," they
keep on repeating. But the absence of wind means that at least
they do not have to take the possible effect of a gust into consideration. Once the bleeding has eased they go behind each one and
wipe his tongue with the soft leaves. They still insist on his spitting right into the fire lest even the minutest particle of blood be
swallowed.

Immediately the specialist drinks copious draughts of coconut
fluid so that any contamination will be drained away quickly with

his urine. He also rubs his hands with the sap of a certain tree to cause sloughing of the skin. It comes up first in a painless rash of blisters.

An hour or so later he prepares a magical potion (*karag*) of the pounded red Cordyline leaves mixed with coconut fluid. This mixture is to encourage healing, and he tells the boys to swill their mouths and expel the liquid into the fire.

Next the assistants light fires in the hut. All retire—specialist, assistants, and boys—but none may sleep, eat, or drink. The boys must not speak, and they must keep their tongues poking out. In addition, everyone is obliged to observe the normal *rekareka* taboos.

At daylight specialist and assistants leave one by one for the sea to perform the *sara* rite and induce menstruation. Before reentering the hut, they smear their bodies with streaks of charcoal in the design called *rekareka*, which indicates the second day of their being set apart. Later they prepare a few tiny rolls of pounded raw breadfruit—so small as to be referred to as rat's excrement. They place some of these in each boy's mouth for his breakfast but eat nothing themselves.

The following day begins with the men incising the penis a second time and changing the charcoal design to another called *wiawia*. They then roast enough breadfruit for a light meal for the boys, who eat it with a fork. The men eat nothing at all but are allowed to suck coconut fluid through a straw.

The third sunrise, on the morning of the fourth day, ends the heaviest of the boys' restrictions. They can now roast their own breadfruit and eat them without a fork, drink water, and scratch as they please. The men, on the other hand, have three extra days to go. They are no longer subject to the worst privations—total fasting, for instance, is not now demanded—but they may eat only a little food, using a fork, drink only coconut fluid, and scratch only with a bone. They refer constantly to enduring such pain, hunger, and thirst and how they expect that in the years to come the boys will make a fitting repayment with offers of daily assistance.

During this time life in the village goes on as usual. Male relatives may approach to within a few yards of the hut and enquire how everyone is faring, but they do not remain long. The older youths bring loads of breadfruit and coconuts and dump them outside. Females are not supposed to be informed about what is happening, though the fact that the older girls take obsidian flakes and make cuts on one another's shoulders suggests that they may have a rough idea. They are said to be suffering "out of sympathy for the boys' mothers."

At the end of the week, on the seventh day, one or both of the village headmen summon the *nibek* monsters, and the men and older youths carry the flutes to the hut where the boys are waiting. The specialist and a couple of his assistants then set out for the forest to obtain quantities of ginger and various leaves and barks for a series of magical potions. These the specialist brews with coconut fluid in a row of holes in the ground, each one lined with leaves of the giant taro plant. The set as a whole is called *matak-walaua*, but the holes are named after particular culture heroes. In Dap Nat Karamwang comes first, with ginger as the principal ingredient, "to restore the boys' warmth"; next comes Wonka, made with the crushed bark of the long smooth aerial roots of the lofty *wonka* variety of Ficus, "to make them tall and clear-skinned"; then there is Malaun, with mashed red Cordyline "to replace the blood"; and so on. The specialist decorates the sides with brightly colored Croton leaves and red and yellow fruits. In Dap the Wonka hole has pride of place, and to it he adds boar's tusks, shell rings, cowrie shells, and other ornaments. He then takes a male and a female flute and passes along the line dipping the ends successively into every potion. He calls the boys up in pairs, one from each moiety, to crouch and take a deep draught, beginning at Nat Karamwang and going on down to the end. Some of the beverages are bitter, some nauseating, and to be certain that the lads do as they are told he keeps his finger in the liquid as they drink and watches the level descend. The last pair —or the last boy alone if there is an odd number of candidates— has to finish every drop.

The men and older youths now collect the boys and, bearing the flutes, direct them to the forest. They seek out all the *wonka* Ficus trees, slash some of the unblemished aerial roots in half, and, holding the sides apart, send the boys through the holes one after

the other. Lofty stature and freedom from skin disease are thus
made doubly certain. They return to the beach laden with more
breadfruit and coconuts.

During the remainder of the seclusion, while the boys are
assiduously practicing on the flutes, the specialist from each of the
surrounding communities brews his set of magical potions to
promote their well-being. It is said that by the end they will have
consumed some portion of every useful tree, creeper, or plant
found on the island. If so, the number is considerable, for the small
children were always telling me that only two forms of vegetation
are valueless. Neighbors accompany their specialist with further
gifts of breadfruit and coconuts.

When the flute-playing becomes monotonous, the boys take a
few hours off to cut sheets of bark, which they scrape and make
into corselets. They like to give the specialist and assistants one
apiece as a token of their gratitude. The men's task considered
specially appropriate is carving new hand drums and slit
gongs.

At length, with the new moon, the *nibek* monsters are sent
away, and the boys reenter the village in a small ceremonial
procession similar to that concluding the earlier rites, when they
first became acquainted with the flutes. But the specialist and the
assistants are still subject to taboos. For a month they must remain
inside the club and cook their own food; in the next month they
can go outside during the day but are not allowed to work or to
eat food prepared by any but a male or a very old woman assumed
to be past sexual intercourse; in the third month they still sleep
in the club but may do any kind of work except planting taro and
eat any kind of food; and in the fourth month they may return
home and begin planting, though sexual intercourse is banned till
the next new moon.

Incising the Penis

Young people in Wogeo are sexually promiscuous before marriage, and the elders therefore warn the boy from the time of his
tongue scarification onwards of the physical risks attendant upon
indulgence. Thus he is fully aware of his need to know how to set

about incising the penis. On this occasion he does not have to wait until his companions are ready. His father may arrange with a kinsman to demonstrate what to do, but it is always possible for the boy himself to take the initiative. Probably the majority have had the instruction by the age of eighteen, though some delay for a year or two longer. The person selected as the teacher is never a close relative—not an uncle or a brother—and this time he is always of the moiety opposite to that of the pupil. Often he comes from a neighboring village.

The two catch a small crab, and each breaks off a sharp claw. They walk to a secluded beach, strip, and wade out till the water reaches their knees. The elder now operates on himself, explaining the procedures as he goes. He watches while the boy imitates his actions and is not satisfied unless the wounds are so deep that the blood gushes forth. Afterwards they are *rekareka* and have to spend a few days in the clubhouse.

Assuming Adult Headdress

Many of the seniors still shave the forehead and push their back hair through a wicker cone (*waro*), giving the effect of a fuzzy mop on a short handle.[3] Generally the cone is well smeared with red ochre and sewn with small cowrie shells around the edges and a row of dogs' teeth at the top. This headgear is adopted during the final initiation rite, when the boy at last attains manhood. To this day the youths submit to the ceremony without complaint—they look upon it as a public acceptance of their status. But afterwards they take the cone off and refuse to wear it, not because of any discomfort that results, but simply on account of their feeling that strangers acquainted with the more sophisticated outside world might label them as still primitive savages.

The celebrations conclude with a feast, and, in consequence, the arrangements have again to be left to the community leaders, who alone can spare the several pigs necessary for a distinguished

---

[3]Formerly men shaved with a flake of volcanic glass obtained from the mainland (the ultimate source was probably the central north coast of New Britain, the area round Talasea). Today they use either a fragment of bottle glass or a razor blade.

Janggara, one of the two headmen of Gol village.

showing. It follows that, as so often was the case previously, there is a delay until one of them has a son of the right age. By then there are other lads waiting, and all go through at once.

On this occasion responsibility for the candidate rests with the senior paternal uncle, who, of course, belongs to the opposite moiety. But if this man is already dead, any patrilateral kinsman may replace him, including a son, necessarily a member of the same moiety as the candidate. The sponsor's first duty is to weave a cone, or to obtain one, sufficiently large at the base to enclose all the youth's hair.

On the day appointed the crowd assembles on the beach, and each sponsor takes his ward into the water. He ducks and scrubs him "to wash away the past" and then has him pulled ashore by a spear entwined in his hair "to encourage further growth." Now he takes the boy's head on his knee and combs and teases the hair into the cone, often bringing on a severe headache. Both eat hot curry served by the women of the village, and afterwards relatives come along with shell and feather decorations.

No taboos are imposed, but for the next few months little work is expected of the candidate. As a rule he avoids the gardens, but he may if he wishes accompany a fishing expedition, though he then protects his head with a twist of palm spathe. Once or twice some older companions conduct him to the forest and there, as before, send him through the aerial roots of a *wonka* Ficus tree, again with the intention of accelerating his growth and enhancing the beauty of his skin. He and his blood brother also go to the mountain stream and drink water together. Relatives in neighboring villages frequently invite him on visits and present him with

Striking the sounding boards (the *nibek's* bone) as the pigs arrive for the feast accompanying an initiation.

food delicacies. His mother's senior brother, or an elder so classified, may even kill a pig in his honor.

As the hair grows, so the sponsor replaces one cone with another, each narrower and taller than the last. Finally, when the ends of the hair appear over the top of a cone some ten inches long, the headman calls up the *nibek* monsters to act as barbers. After the sponsor has trimmed the young man's locks to fit a cone of ordinary size the feast is prepared. The food is shared among the men and eaten on the beach. The monsters are then sent home, and the candidate emerges as a fully initiated responsible citizen ready to shoulder the burdens of marriage and the rearing of a family.

VI Menstruation and Childbirth

First Menstruation

Girls pass through but one initiation rite, at the menarche. No institution corresponding with the men's club requires their formal admission in successive stages, and no ceremony takes place to mark the end of their infancy or the middle of their childhood. A father operates on his daughter's ear lobes whenever he happens to feel so inclined—perhaps if a rainy day has confined the family to the house—and a mother is equally casual in providing a first garment. She may deck the child out to show her off to relatives while the little thing can still barely walk, but wait for five or ten more years before expecting her to be dressed all the time.

Although the single rite is in many respects similar to tongue scarification, it is less elaborate. The reason is simple. In the first place, the Wogeo world is man made. Then, unlike the boy, a girl's maturity is immediately obvious, and for this reason a group of girls, some older, some younger, cannot be put through together. A further difference arises from the fact that it is considered proper to lay greater emphasis on promoting physical attractiveness than growth.

First menstruation occurs later in New Guinea than among ourselves. Two girls just learning to walk when I arrived in 1934 on my earlier visit had menstruated immediately prior to my return during 1948, when they must have been fifteen; and I know of others who could not have been younger than sixteen or seventeen. The father likes to have enough food on hand for feasting, and generally he takes the precaution of planting extra gardens as soon as the event appears to be imminent. If caught unawares, and if he cannot easily borrow—as, for example, when his brothers are saving for a celebration of some kind on their own account—he may tell his wife to keep the girl in the house until the deficiency is remedied, perhaps as much as six months later. One man found his daughter's initial period so inconvenient that he ignored it and, when she menstruated again, he and his wife pretended that nothing had happened before.

Marigum's second daughter, Magar, menstruated within a month of my reaching Dap. He and I were one morning talking together under a tree in a quiet corner of the village, and as he spoke no pidgin English and I at that time had barely mastered a sentence of the local language, his son Tafalti, Magar's full brother, was acting as an interpreter. By a coincidence we were discussing the menstrual rite in general terms, and he had mentioned that I might be seeing one in the near future. Suddenly his senior wife, Yam, approached. "It's come," she announced. "Magar's just told me. She's sitting there weeping now." "I've been telling Hogbin she was about due," he replied. "Well, I'm ready. Go ahead with everything." He then bade a youth who was passing to inform the women already at work in the cultivations so that as many as possible might return.

Magar's mother had died several years before, and Yam, as the chief of the remaining wives, stepped into her place. I later discovered that there was little affection between stepmother and stepdaughter, but throughout these proceedings the older woman's behavior was impeccable. She did all that might have been expected of a true mother for a beloved offspring.

Marigum and Tafalti made no move towards Magar. They denied any fear of direct contact with her, serious though the consequences would be during all her later periods, and insisted simply that they could not be bothered with women's affairs—a statement that later events were to prove incorrect. As for her crying, that was to be expected. Every girl wept at this early sign of her approaching marriage and departure from the family home, but who knew whether the thought gave her pain or pleasure? Perhaps the tears might also be connected with embarrassment at having to play a leading part in the forthcoming ceremonial.

Soon several housewives arrived back from the gardens and

began cooking vegetable curry. Before the dish was ready for serving, a few of the senior women conducted Magar to the beach for a bath. They scrubbed her thoroughly, and Yam produced a new garment cut with the four fringes that would mark the attainment of adulthoood. Subsequently while menstruating Magar would have to dress in plain black or brown, but this skirt was white. Yam also twisted a palm spathe over the girl's head and wrapped a plaited mat around her shoulders. These Magar wore till the end of the ceremonies. The head covering was to prevent the premature greying of her hair, the mat to give protection from the roughening effect of the sun's hot rays (the fact that exposure also increases pigmentation was not mentioned; indeed, the people deny any special preference for a light coloring).

Once the toilet was complete, the party retired to Marigum's house. Here Yam gave Magar a bone scratcher, and her sister-in-law, the girl's paternal aunt, gave her a bone fork for eating. Both women warned of the taboo on touching the body with the nails and on eating with the fingers. Other prohibitions apply to the consumption of raw food, chewing betelnut, and smoking. But a girl at her first menstruation, unlike a boy at his, does not have to refrain from drinking water, though before doing so she must tip it out of the container into a coconut-shell cup. Still another variation is that, although the curry is served piping hot to counteract the ritual coldness as well as the real chill that everyone agrees is inevitable in her condition, she is not permitted to warm herself by approaching the fire. It is accepted that the external heat would be comforting, but the flames have to be avoided—like the direct rays of the sun—lest her flesh should become wasted and her beauty thereby impaired.

The village women now entered with platters of curry, and all ate a good meal. Then, after a short rest, they departed for the forest, where Magar, amid much merriment, was persuaded to pass through several of the split roots of *wonka* fig trees. The object was the same as in the similar ceremony for the boys—to preserve her smooth skin.

Next morning a pair of older girls who expected to be menstruating in the near future presented themselves on the verandah of Marigum's house to be Magar's companions, her *kirigirig*, until

the rite was concluded. Yam immediately made them welcome
with breakfast. Normally, there are three or four *kirigirig*, but
these two were the only ones of the right age in the entire district.
The elder, who was from Dap, did menstruate eight months later,
but the other, from Kinaba, matured more slowly. It was their job
to accompany Magar everywhere, to sleep with their arms round
her to keep her warm, to wash her each day, and to supply her
with leaves of the *bulima* plant to chew so that her teeth would
go black, regarded as another mark of beauty. They carried her
scratcher and fork wherever they went and adjusted her head
covering and cloak as often as was necessary. When in her presence, they observed the taboos to which she was subject, though
they did so out of sympathy and politeness rather than for ritual
reasons. Thus I saw one of them excuse herself and go behind a
bush before giving her itchy scalp a good scratch.

Later in the day Magar and these companions went to Yam's
gardens and began weeding them. Soon they were joined by the
village women, who for a short time helped with the work. Then
one of them began singing, and all took up the chorus. The tasks
were quickly forgotten, and they played games and generally
enjoyed themselves, with a great deal of noise, till well into the
afternoon. They then retired to the settlement, where the men
had set out piles of coconuts, areca nuts, betel pepper, and tobacco.
The housewives prepared pots of food, and the proceedings ended
with a small feast. Magar and the companions received the choic-
est morsels and were the center of attention. Wild taro and cooking bananas, for instance, though not injurious to them, were felt
to be inappropriate in their present state.

Next day a headman's wife from Kinaba invited the girls to
weed her gardens, and the events were repeated. A few young
women from Dap accompanied them, and those from Kinaba
came along to help. Again they all sang, played games, and afterwards feasted. Over the following fortnight similar calls arrived
from other villages in the vicinity, and there were festivities on
practically every fine afternoon.

Magar was honored more than if she had been the daughter of
an ordinary householder. As a rule, only about four outside invita-
tions are received, and they are from such close relatives as the

paternal and maternal aunts. Fewer women attend, and there is less food.

Now came the brewing of magical potions for the girls to drink, each potion aimed at enhancing their grace and good looks. No woman has the necessary brewing skill, and three men volunteered, all close relatives of Magar. They had inherited this knowledge along with that to make the similar beverages for the boys. They sought out the vegetable substances in the bush and then proceeded to the beach, calling the girls to follow. Many of the women went to watch. Magar drank first, then the companions. The bystanders saluted each mouthful with loud acclaim. The entire ceremony was quickly over, and within half an hour everyone was back in the village.

The weaving of the rattan bands on Magar's waist, wrists, arms, and ankles now began. The companions spread a mat in a shady spot in the village, bade her sit on it, and various of her male relatives approached with needles and bundles of dried cane. I have mentioned how tedious the task is and that it demands good eyesight and constant attention. As one man became tired, so another took over for half an hour or so. Sometimes a collar is also woven, but for Magar this was omitted. Even so, the work took well over three hours without counting the time spent on the much narrower bands for the wrists of the companions. By then supper was nearly ready, but before it could be served Magar's paternal aunt descended and, with a piece of broken glass, trimmed the hair of the three girls. She shaved the back of their necks, cut the straggling ends above the ears, and straightened the line over their foreheads.

Early in the morning Yam and the other older housewives sent the unmarried girls and some of the younger women not yet encumbered with children to the top of the mountain behind Dap to clear away the brushwood from the spot where a ceremony would take place on the morrow. Magar and the companions accompanied them, again passing through roots on the way, but on arrival they sat in the shade resting and singing. Soon the others came over, and all played games till the early afternoon.

Meantime the women left behind in the village busied themselves making a quantity of coconut oil. They broke dried nuts open, cut the flesh into small chips, wrapped these in leaves, and baked them on hot stones till the liquid came oozing out. This they caught in the fibrous gauze stripped off a palm tree. The sticky mess, when squeezed, yielded drops of the clarified oil. That evening, when the young people returned, each woman produced a greasy bundle and anointed Magar and the companions on the forehead. Yam came last, carrying instead a coconut shell of red ochre, which she smeared on the oil.

During the afternoon Marigum and some of the headmen from places nearby had told a few of the youths to take some flutes from the club into the surrounding forest and there play a few tunes so that the monsters might appear to be paying their respects to Magar as his daughter. Had she been the child of an ordinary householder the spirits would not have been expected to give heed to what was going on.

Now came the day of the celebrations on the mountain top. After a hurried meal before dawn, Magar, the companions, and the other girls sallied forth for the climb to the center of the island. The women from Dap and the places nearby came on with baskets laden with food, oil, and paint after they had fed the children and finished the morning tasks in and around the house.

The first business was the committal of Magar's childhood to the grave, and to begin with everyone conducted herself with mock solemnity. In imitation of real mourners, they donned a head covering made from a twisted palm spathe to protect their hair and smeared their bodies with dirt to indicate sorrow. Yam brought out an old black petticoat practically in rags to represent the corpse, and in front of this they all wept and wailed and smote their bosoms in an agony of assumed sorrow. Each woman addressed the bundle by the appropriate kinship term as though it had in fact been Magar's child—"Alas, you have left us, my grandchild; I shall see you no more," "My dear little sister, why should you have chosen to become a spirit so soon," and so forth. Then two or three scraped out a hole, and, amid an ecstasy of lamentations, the skirt was interred.

Next Yam threw away Magar's head covering and cloak, and the women painted her and the companions. Those from Dap produced the oil, those from the places round about coconut half-shells filled with red ochre. They anointed the three all over, including their hair, then squeezed more oil into the paint pots and smeared them well with the mixture till it was literally dropping from their bodies.[1]

Various women now offered gifts of brightly colored feathers, dogs' teeth, shell rings, and other ornaments obtained from their husbands. These were decorations for Magar, and, as a mark of her father's being a headman, Yam picked out a couple of boars' tusks. She stuck the feathers in the girl's greasy hair and hung the other things in her armbands or round her neck.

The meal followed and then general games, with the usual noise and horseplay.

I should explain that I had wanted to be there, but the men expressed such disapproval when I said so that I had no alternative but to delay until I could come on the scene legitimately in male company later. "We've told you, this is just the concern of women," my friends exclaimed. "You'd look a fool sitting there alone with them—that is, if they let you; but probably they'd beat you up and drive you away. Besides, it's all nonsense, nothing to take seriously." What seemed to upset them was the conviction that the goings on were inspired by a desire to make fun of men's secrets and male superiority. I had no means of discovering whether the men's suspicions were well founded, but they assured me with distaste that there would be lewd imitations of the *lewa* dances; some wives would cause laughter by simulating the gait, gestures, and speech mannerisms of the husbands; and others, fastening a banana and coconuts to their skirts, would ridicule the male anatomy.

The sound of the shrieking, borne on the wind, was clearly audible in the village, and soon the younger men and youths were making known their profound irritation. They objected to the women's being so blatant in asserting enjoyment. "I'm deafened," said one, grossly exaggerating, as he waved his fist in the air. "They ought to be planting taro or weeding instead of gallivanting up there. It's disgraceful." Had I not been aware that every-

---

[1]Men when painting mix the ingredients differently. They hold a pinch of ochre in the left hand, tip a drop or two of oil on it, and then rub the palms together.

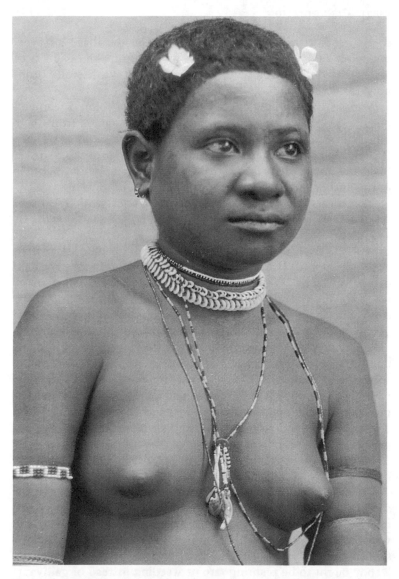

Magar

thing was taking place according to the accepted pattern I might
have assumed that an unexpected feminist upsurge was in pro-

gress and the males were resisting the loss of traditional privileges.

At about ten o'clock one of the men called out, "Come, my brothers. This can't go on any longer. No more delay. We'll go together and drive them home." Off we all marched, each telling his comrades how angry he was. Unfortunately, as we advanced a light rain set in, and our arrival was an anticlimax. The women, instead of running about, were quietly sheltering under the trees waiting. We did our best to strike terror into them, nevertheless, by yelling, pushing, brandishing switches of leaves, and flinging handfuls of mud. We carefully avoided molesting Magar and the companions, but nobody gave a thought to the rule that the persons of the opposite moiety must be respected, and a few suffered minor cuts and bruises. Soon they were in retreat down the steep slopes, with us in hot pursuit.

In normal circumstances the women would have had a feast that afternoon, but the rain was now coming down too heavily for comfort out of doors, and it was decided to wait till the next day.

This last feast is known as "the ashes" or "the dead embers" (jim), partly because it comes at the close of the ceremonies, partly because the food is considered to be a repayment to the women who have labored over the cooking fires to make the celebrations a success.[2] On this occasion Magar's relatives on both sides provided the bulk of the supplies, but, out of respect for her father's status, extra contributions came from the residents of the neighboring villages. Marigum provided dried fish, sago, and bananas, the rest taro and yams. The bananas were made into a dish called taf, which is always prepared by men, though women alone eat it. The fruit is boiled, mashed, mixed with an equal quantity of grated coconut, rolled, cut, and rolled again into small cakes, which are served on leaves. Magar's consumption of some of these cakes marked the end of her observance of the food taboos.

Had the feast been held at the usual time the women would not have painted Magar again, but as by now the pigment had begun

---

[2] A man rewards those who have helped him to construct a new canoe or weave a new hunting net with three feasts. The first is "the ashes" (jim) and is ostensibly intended for the women who have cooked food for the workers; the second, "the platters" (kalog), is for both the workers and their wives; the third, "the reef heron" (tariga), is for the men only. At first menstruation "the platters" and "the reef heron" are omitted.

to rub off and look untidy, they approached with their oil and shells of ochre and redecorated her and the companions before beginning to peel the vegetables and heat the fires.

Work started early in the afternoon, and, following the regular routine for feasting, men and women labored together. They finished at about four, when the housewives from Kinaba, Job, and elsewhere drifted in with their bowls and baskets. The first ceremony opened with one of the senior men kindling a fire in the center of the village. When it was fully alight, but not blazing, the companions took each of Magar's hands as she stepped over it, back and forth, several times. They then stood for a few minutes in the smoke. I gathered that this ceremony was a ritual fumigation, a burning out of any unhealthy supernatural influences. I do not know of anything similar taking place on other occasions. The same elder then bade the three stand in line nearby, and several youths, bearing the bowls of food, encircled them three times, traveling in a counterclockwise direction. This exercise echoed that carried out when the youths emerged from seclusion after the cutting of their tongues.

A short ceremony for the women followed. Nobody could explain its purpose, though it is always performed. I have no theory about why it should be regarded as significant, and possibly it is little more than another expression of lighthearted fun. One of the senior housewives came out of her dwelling carrying a long dried pandanus leaf such as is used for mat making. She held it over her head and began chanting the air sung by the crew trying out a new canoe: "The streamer flutters from the top of the mast; it flutters and rustles in the wind; it flutters, rustles, flutters, rustles, flutters, rustles all the way from our island to the open sea and back again." The other women took up the tune and formed a long chain behind her. Round and round Magar they went for about ten minutes. Then they seized hot taro corms and threw them to one another over her head.

Yam now came to the front and suggested that they carry the food to the beach. Off they went, leaving the men behind, and arranged the bowls in an open place above the high-water mark. Then a fracas began just like that preceding the men's feast, with Magar and the companions safely behind a tree. Wives made for

interfering sisters-in-law, jealous spouses for the husbands' suspected mistresses, and so on, I saw none of it, again because my
men friends dissuaded me; but next morning several of the participants were disfigured, one with a black eye and half a dozen with
long scratches on the cheeks or arms. Suddenly Yam rushed in
and hurled bunches of areca nuts in all directions. This was the
signal to stop. "Now we've had our own *nibek,*" the combatants
were alleged to have remarked as they smiled at one another.

The men were ostentatious in paying no attention. For the rest
of the day not one of them so much as referred to what was going
on only fifty yards away behind a screen of trees. They chatted
about their gardens and pigs, forthcoming events, proposed overseas voyages, and a dozen other matters, making no gesture of
anger even when the noise rose in a crescendo and we could
barely hear ourselves speaking. Next day, in response to my enquiries, they remarked that they supposed that the women's conduct was as bad as it had been on the mountain top. One elderly
woman, another of Magar's stepmothers, had launched a canoe,
yelling out, so a neighbor told me, that, fed up with the small
penes available in Wogeo, she intended to migrate to the mainland
in search of a man skilled in copulation; and two other respectable
mothers of families had given a hilarious demonstration of mutual
masturbation, driven to doing so, they declared, by the inade-
quacy of their husbands. "I clouted my own wife when she came
home. I won't have her scorning us men in that fashion," he
concluded. Several other householders seem to have followed this
example.

All that remained to be done was for Magar and the companions to bathe and drink the waters in the hills. They went off in
the morning, making for the stream used by male initiands. They
avoided the topmost pool, however, and took the one immediately
below it, underneath a small cascade. No married woman was
present, only a handful of girls a year or two older than themselves. These instructed them in what to do. First Magar had to
drink, calling the name of each companion in turn with two
phrases afterwards, "my *bulima* leaf, my yam leaf" (as was mentioned, the companions kept her supplied with *bulima* leaves to
turn her teeth black). She thereby entered into a bond of blood

sisterhood, accepting obligations corresponding with those between blood brothers. Then the attendants told her to put away her scratcher and fork and to sit in the water for a good wash.

The youths were in the forest with the flutes as the party descended toward home. In the village the Dap women and those from outside whose gardens Magar had weeded were waiting with bowls of food and bundles of sweet-smelling herbs, which they tucked into her armbands. All the females of the village joined in the meal, and now at last Magar was considered to have grown up.

Until a few years ago, if the girl having her first menstruation was already betrothed, her younger male relatives came to meet her as she approached the village on the way from the stream. At the edge of the settlement the male relatives of her promised bridegroom intercepted the group and attempted to abduct her, never with success. After a few minutes her father and the father of the boy ran into the melee with orders to stop. Later they combined in entertaining the participants. The custom has now been abandoned.

Menstruation Later

A girl does not become regular immediately, and several months may elapse before she has a second period. The only thing out of the ordinary then is that the mother cooks her a bowl of curry and advises her to lie near the fire; otherwise she now starts taking the precautions that all menstruating women are expected to observe. First, to make her condition known to all, she replaces her white or colored skirt with one dyed black or dark brown. After that, the keynote of her behavior is avoidance. She does not appear to be embarrassed and is allowed to speak freely and join in conversation, but she has to refrain from physical contact with other people. (Equally, other people are expected to refrain from physical contact with her—that is why she advertises her condition with the dun-colored skirt. It is agreed that one menstruating female is unlikely to contaminate another, but they still keep their distance.) She does not touch anyone else or anyone else's belongings; when leaving or entering the house she passes through a hole in the floor or wall, not the doorway; when obliged to visit the cultivations she stays in her own gardens; when hungry she cooks for herself; when thirsty she sucks the liquid through a straw; when eating she holds the food with a fork; and when itchy she takes a scratcher.

Childbirth

A parturient woman is not considered to be a source of danger yet, and if the child will be her first, the mother, mother-in-law, and one or two other older housewives of experience are in constant attendance even before the pains begin. The peril starts at the actual moment of birth, and from then to the next full moon she is subject to the various taboos. As an extra protection she is secluded in a special hut (*bwaruka*) that her husband (or brothers if she is unmarried) has erected in readiness out of any old timber lying around the village. The floor is always raised above the ground, and the builder makes certain that the walls and roof, however flimsy, are proof against the rain. The usual dimensions are about six feet square by six feet high. Inside there is a wild-palm spathe to serve as a bed, a fireplace, and a pile of fuel.

The precise location of the hut depends on whether the household includes any very young children who are likely to go seeking their mother. Should this be so the building is hidden deep in the forest at some distance from the settlement, and the grown-ups say that she has gone on a visit to relatives. On her return she informs the youngsters that she found the baby nestling in a cave with a flock of flying foxes. But for a firstborn such extreme care is unnecessary, and the man erects the shelter a few yards from the rear of the dwelling. (In early married life the woman may want to have the infant near her old home, but the husband's relatives and her own try to discourage her, and more often than not they succeed.)

With the onset of labor, the relatives help the women to a secluded section of the beach. They strew leaves thickly to make a rough couch and then assist as best they can. They hold mats over her as protection from the rain or the sun, support her back, press on her shoulders, and so on. But with the delivery they step back and keep their hands to themselves. One of them immediately announces the sex of the child to the men waiting in the village—short sharp calls for a male and a long-drawn halloo for a female. All this time the husband participates by keeping indoors and opening every box, loosening every bundle, and untying every knot.

Ritual considerations effectively prevent attempts to correct a malpresentation by manipulation, and if the labor is unduly prolonged the attendants have only magic to fall back on. They send word to the husband, begging him to go over the boxes, bundles, and cords and make doubly sure that nothing has been missed, and if this fails to bring relief they appeal to a specialist in the magic known as "the spate" (*dan-sauasaua*, literally "water flowing strongly"). He recites a spell over a vessel of water, which he then sends to the beach with instructions to allow the contents to trickle over the woman's abdomen. They may go on trying such specialists until the baby is born or the woman dies.

After a successful delivery the mother rests for a few minutes to regain her strength and then cuts the cord with a bamboo knife —even today steel is never used. She gathers up the afterbirth and the bloody leaves and throws everything into the sea, washes herself and the infant in salt water, and staggers with it to the hut, where a kinswoman will have lit a fire and arranged the bed. The other women, after watching to see that she is safe, prepare her a dish of stewed figs, which she has to eat at once. From then until she returns to the village, they and her other relatives keep her supplied with food, firewood, and water. As usual, she eats with a fork, drinks through a straw, and uses a scratcher.

A stillborn infant, or one that is premature, is disposed of with the afterbirth, but if it dies a day or two later the woman wraps the body in a mat and places it in a basket, which she gives to her husband for burial deep in the forest. He avoids touching the dead flesh and thus has no need to perform a ceremony of purification.

Nearly always the woman manages to reach the hut, but if she stumbles and falls there is a strong chance that someone will come to her aid—her mother, mother-in-law, a sister or a sister-in-law —even though this person ought also to be subject to the taboos. When Burua went to help her husband's sister Mwago, however, she stayed in the hut for two days only and then returned to her family. On my expressing astonishment at such indiscretion the relatives excused her conduct by pointing out that, with four children, her responsibilities were urgent; moreover, they insisted that the patient had now recovered. On another occasion I saw four older women carrying a mother to the hut on a rough stretcher. Each had covered her hands with rags to prevent any chance of defilement.

If a woman dies in childbirth or shortly afterwards while still secluded, the traditional mourning is omitted, and the husband and her brothers bury the body at once without any outside help.

The child itself, once washed, is not taboo, and the grandmothers and the aunts are, after a couple of days, permitted to hold it for a few minutes at a time. The mother places it on the bed, and they pick it up from there without touching her. No man will ever handle a baby, but the father may come along to look at his offspring from a distance. As yet he abstains from working lest the blows from his axe break its sinews, and for two or three weeks he stays near the village. He and the rest of the household eat normal meals, nevertheless, prepared by an older girl or sent in by neighbors.

People now discuss possible names for the child, or rather, which of the ancestors ought to be commemorated. The paternal and the maternal grandfather have the right to choose one each (if they are dead, the senior paternal and maternal uncles), but as a rule the maternal grandfather exercises his privilege only for the eldest son and the eldest daughter, and even then his choice of name is seldom heard. The ceremony takes place as soon as a decision has been reached. The relatives assemble, and the paternal grandfather, or the senior paternal uncle, or the father himself, in a loud voice repeats the names of as many of his forbears as he can remember. When he reaches the one selected the kinsfolk call out, "Yes, the child is Such-and-such." An assistant then breaks a green coconut that he has been holding in readiness, and the man takes a mouthful of the fluid and spits it out in a fine spray on the crowd. Later he splits a stalk of ginger and hangs the pieces on the front of his house.

On the morning of the day after the full moon the woman pulls down the hut, flings the boards into the sea, and goes back to her dwelling. To celebrate the resumption of everyday living she cooks a taro corm for each of the men in the community and a dish of crabs to be shared among the members of her own sex.

Two details remain. On the appearance of the second new moon she takes the baby to her husband's headman so that he can carry out magic for its well-being, and a little later, with the same object in view, she gives him the umbilical cord to dispose of in deep water far out to sea "so that it may never shrivel and dry out."

VII   Illness and Death

We have seen how religious belief provides the means whereby people convince themselves that hazardous enterprises can be brought to successful conclusion. Artificial menstruation is an essential preliminary to anyone's joining in a raid or trading expedition and to his helping in the manufacture of a new sail for an overseas canoe or a new hunting net. Ritually purified, he feels alert and full of vigor; and hence he is confident of his ability to cope with the possible difficulties and dangers ahead. In the present chapter I propose to consider the place of belief in the crises of illness and death. Briefly, belief offers the patient a course of procedures ostensibly practical; and if in spite of the maneuvers he succumbs, it then presents the survivors with moral justification for action or for inaction according to choice. With perfect propriety they can either select someone as responsible for the death and kill him, or, when this would be unwise, put forward a valid excuse for doing nothing.

The Young and the Old

Children's sicknesses are treated differently from those of their seniors, and it will be well to deal with them first. A single paragraph will suffice. The infant-mortality rate is high in Wogeo, and only about half the babies survive to reach puberty. A common assumption is that an envious ghost has snatched the child's soul and that the immature body is unable to withstand the shock. Vengeance cannot be projected beyond the grave, however, and the ghost perforce remains unpunished. A parent may sometimes

141

complain that really a sorcerer was at work, but the other relatives are never prepared to agree. They insist that someone so tiny could not possibly have given offense.

The procedure adopted when at length the aged breathe their last also fails to conform to the general pattern. Again the closest kinsmen may talk of sorcery, even of their determination to be avenged, but the rest will have none of it. Their view is that in such a situation death is natural and ought to be accepted with equanimity as the final stage of senility. "This is the way we all ought to go—to continue till the body is worn out, like an axe thrown away when there is no point in trying to sharpen it further," I heard a man explain to his children after their grandmother's funeral. "Were it not for sorcery none of us here in Wogeo would ever be struck down while still capable of a day's work. Death should be the slipping away of everything—disintegration —first the firmness of the flesh, then the teeth, then the strength in the arms and the legs, then the understanding, and at the end the breath."

Thus it seems that the loss of the very young and the very old, despite the feelings of the bereaved family, is not considered to be of concern to the community as a whole. The young have not yet developed a social personality, and the aged have been parted from theirs by the gradual process of physical decay.

Normal Reaction to Illness

Ordinarily a person who is feeling poorly begins turning over in his (or her) mind whether during the previous month or so he may have without good reason been on garden land belonging to some other group. Should he recall doing so, he confesses the fault and expresses regret to one of the owners, requesting this man also to intercede with the living culture heroes who have been offended. A return to good health means that the apology has been accepted. But if instead the patient's condition continues to deteriorate, then he realizes the urgency of seeking another explanation. It may be that a ghost has stolen some of his soul stuff and hot curry will effect a cure. Or perhaps, for a male victim, artificial menstruation has been delayed too long; if so, he at once sets about performing the *sara* bleeding operation. Most commonly, however, the sickness is attributed to sorcery

Sorcery to cause illness only is distinct from sorcery aimed at killing the victim. Various ailments are recognized; for example, toothache, headache, abdominal pain, boils, tropical ulcers, colds, sore throat, cough, diarrhea, malaria, conjunctivitis, swollen testes, blood in the urine, and tenderness in the joints—all have special names. Each is associated with a magical system that includes rites to induce the complaint and rites to alleviate it. Every member of the community has a knowledge of at least one system; moreover, he does not attempt to conceal the fact. The villagers are thus aware of which of their neighbors can inflict them with a particular disease and also relieve its symptoms. This one can cause and cure toothache, that one headache, a third bellyache, and so on. Strictly speaking, the harmful rites should be reserved solely for the protection of property from thieves (*bwab* magic), but in practice they are employed just as often to punish offenders, known or alleged (*muj* magic).

I have already explained that close relatives are mutually dependent, especially those living together in the one housing cluster. The heavier tasks demand cooperation, and even on other occasions most people prefer working together for the sake of the company. It follows that an open quarrel between neighbors is something of a disaster. The one refuses to assist the other, and hence both are losers. There is a risk also that soon the community itself will be split asunder. Such catastrophes are best avoided, as everyone knows, by those with grievances concealing their feelings. Instead of chiding the supposed wrongdoer, they hold their tongues and have recourse to the milder form of sorcery. In public they behave as though cherishing a warm regard for him, while simultaneously in private they bend their endeavors toward making him suffer.

It is important to note that on occasions of this kind death sorcery is normally out of the question. The injured parties, except perhaps in the heat of the moment on first discovering the offense, are fully conscious of the fact that to kill would mean depriving themselves of a valued helper.

The people bathe frequently, but the claims of hygiene are

otherwise ignored, and there is in consequence a good deal of sickness. Thus, in course of time, those who perform disease sorcery always have the satisfaction of seeing their victim under attack or, better still, in agony. They are then sure of their responsibility for what is happening. Though pretending sympathy, they are content to believe that evil has at last met its deserts. Of course, it often happens that the rite for one ailment is followed by the onset of another, but for this an explanation is readily forthcoming. The magic may have worked itself out in a new way, or the spell could have been misquoted and a wrong medicine selected; or there was a doubling-up effect, the result of coincidence, as when the man had attracted the attentions of an additional sorcerer.

The patient, even if he has a guilty conscience, makes no attempt to discover who exactly may have directed the rituals against him. Indeed, it is difficult to see how he might do so. Those whose enmity he had incurred would have been careful to see that their overt behavior aroused no suspicion about what was going on. The sufferer simply approaches one of the several persons who are able to deal with the complaint and submits to the remedies prescribed. A near kinsman is willing to act for nothing, but a consultant brought in from outside, perhaps on account of his superior reputation, expects a small fee. In most cases natural resistance triumphs over the infection, and before long recovery is complete. Restorative magic therefore appears to be no less satisfactory than disease sorcery.

Death

When discussing the problem in the abstract, without anyone specifically in mind, the villagers used to tell me that on the occasions when the cures failed and the sick man or woman perished, then, provided he or she was not already elderly, this fact in itself proved that the members of the bereaved household had mistaken the type of sorcery employed. They ought to have been quick to notice some signs of the lethal kind (*yabou*), though what such signs might have been was never made clear. The proper thing now, people would say, was the performance of an inquest ceremony to identify the culprit. Once the man's name was public property a decision could be taken on the form of vengeance— whether to rely on counter sorcery or to kill him outright with an axe or a spear.

It is insisted also that death by what we would call accident or misadventure is the result of this same kind of lethal sorcery and ought to be avenged. Men go up the tall Canarium trees regularly during the season to gather the harvest, and wives and sisters on the ground are seldom concerned for their safety. Surely then if a climber places his weight on a branch that turns out to be rotten and as a result breaks his neck, the obvious conclusion is that a sorcerer bent on mischief had been along beforehand. Similarly, the vast majority of the trading canoes reach the mainland without incident, but from time to time, despite every magical precaution, one of them founders and the crew is drowned. What other inter-pretation but sorcery is conceivable? Snakebite and goring by a wild boar are the same. It so happened that during my visit a man succumbed to an attack by a deadly taipan or some equally venomous snake. Within the hour his brothers were at my door, but he was dead before I could reach him. The relatives had no difficulty in accepting that the poison injected by the fangs was the immediate cause—the punctures were plainly visible on the foot of the body. Yet they were quite firm in maintaining that a sorcerer had persuaded the reptile to strike. Were there not thou-sands of snakes on Wogeo? And did they not slither out of the way? How else but by sorcery could I explain why this particular snake had behaved against its nature and picked this particular man out as its target?

As is so often the case in Wogeo, however, theory and practice need not coincide. It is safe to take for granted that when a death does occur the immediate relatives of the deceased will insist, at least to begin with, that he or she was slain by *yabou* sorcery; but other people may not share the opinion. They allow that the sons and the brothers, from motives of family loyalty, are bound to clamour about *yabou;* but almost invariably for a woman victim, and more often than not for a man, the hint soon circulates that infringements of the rules regarding menstruation and sexual relations were the more likely causes of destruction. I have discussed at length the taboos surrounding men and women who are menstruating, and mention was also made of the belief that committing adultery with the spouse of a close relative leads to supernatural punishment. The *yabou* explanation is acceptable to a large circle only when a prominent person has died, and as a rule even then revenge by counter sorcery is considered to be sufficient. Killing by outright violence for the practice of primary sorcery probably takes place almost exclusively when the dead man had enjoyed a truly outstanding reputation.

The incidents surrounding the death of Waki in Job village are typical. She was the widow of a noted headman who had died some two years before; but their son, Gwaramun, still in his late twenties, had not yet fully established himself. Perhaps of greater significance socially was an affinal tie with Marigum—Yam, Waki's eldest daughter, was Marigum's favorite wife and the mother of his chosen heir. At the time of the fatal illness Waki was about sixty. Possessed of great self-assurance and an immense dignity, she exercised indirectly a strong influence on Job affairs. The respect in which she was held may be gathered from a note in my diary written a fortnight before the earliest signs of the sickness—"Here is one person whose death will certainly be avenged."

At first Waki's condition gave rise to no great concern. She was confined to the house with pains in the chest and recurrent fits of coughing, but it was assumed that health magic would be effective. Then suddenly she grew worse, and some of the neighbors began expressing the fear that she might be the object of *yabou* sorcery. Several men raised the question of who the guilty person might be, but they did not press enquiries or label anyone in particular. The death a week later confirmed their suspicions, though for the next forty-eight hours everybody was too busy with the funeral arrangements to think much of other things.

From the moment that the body was safely in the grave, the subject of *yabou* became the sole topic of conversation. The closest kin were mourning, and I could not as yet obtain their views, but other people spoke of such matters as how evil sorcerers were and how careful we all must be when traveling about lest we also should be killed; and they tentatively suggested whence the blow might have come. Could it be that a man from Bagiau was to blame? After all, many of the residents there were untrustworthy. Or what about Ga? A Ga headman was well known as an economic rival of Waki's deceased husband—might he not have transferred his envy to her? And there was also Takul to be considered. But it was quite impossible to contemplate that anyone from our own locality was responsible. We were all so closely related, were conscious of each other's inmost thoughts, and would at once have been aware of lurking anger or malice against Waki, of whom we were all so very fond and to whom we all owed so much. Well, we were fortunate. Marigum was familiar with how to conduct an inquest and would not hestiate in bringing the murderer to justice. As soon as the mourners emerged from seclusion he would perform the ceremony, and we would then have our revenge.

In due course I was able to talk to the son and daughter, Gwaramun and Yam. They were in no doubt that their mother had been killed by sorcery and assured me that any day now Marigum would proceed with the inquest. I then approached him myself. I asked when he would be performing the necessary ritual. I was eager to be present and record what was done. He replied that at this period he was too busy but, as I knew well, he would, as always, give me ample notice of his intentions. During the following months I repeated the query over and over again and on each occasion received a new excuse for further delay. He was not feeling well and would wait until he was better; the almond harvest must be completed first; as soon as the weather improved; carrying on business of this kind might affect the annual rising of the palolo worm, due within the month; the District Officer at the Government station on the mainland might come to know and be angry—a European politician could not have glossed over inactivity more adroitly. I have no means of knowing, of course, whether his reactions were predetermined or whether he was improvising as he went along.

Gwaramun and Yam retained their faith till my departure and still talked about what they would do once the guilt had been revealed; but by then the other folk, though discreet with their gossip and always holding their tongues in front of the members of Waki's family, were saying that perhaps their earlier judgement

had been over-hasty. Was it not more likely that a breach of taboo
was behind the death? Two or three of my most intimate helpers
whispered that they remembered hearing from their fathers years
before of a rumored intrigue between Waki and her husband's
brother. One man even added that Marigum, in putting off the
inquest, might be aiming at preserving Waki's reputation. Performance meant incurring the risk that sorcery would be denied, and
the entire population would then know that probably her own
misconduct had brought about her end.

Now let us turn to an investigation of how this lethal form of
sorcery is carried out—or, rather, how it is supposed to be carried
out.[1]

Yabou

I have to admit at the outset that I neither saw the rites performed nor met anyone who would acknowledge having done so.
Many people were prepared to list for my benefit those whom
they suspected were regular practitioners—always the majority of
the names submitted were those of residents of other districts—
but I was warned not to betray the confidence and that I must
never approach any person with such a statement as, "I've been
told you know how to kill with sorcery; do describe what you do."
It follows that the information here set out is based entirely on
hearsay. In general it agrees with that reported from several other
parts of Melanesia, though there are minor differences of detail
from place to place.[2] I shall give what might be considered the
orthodox statement and briefly indicate the points at which opinions conflict.

It should be noted that no attempt is made to explain how a

---

[1]The following section gives but a brief summary of the subject. The full
account is best postponed for inclusion in a later publication.

[2]See, for example, C. G. Seligman, *Melanesians of British New Guinea* (Cam-
bridge 1910), pp. 170–171; B. Malinowski, "Natives of Mailu," *Transactions of the
Royal Society of South Australia*, Vol. 39 (1915), p. 649; R. F. Fortune, *Sorcerers of
Dobu* (London 1932), pp. 234-237; and I. Hogbin, *A Guadalcanal Society* (New York
1963), pp. 56-58. In the East Sepik Administrative District of New Guinea, within
which Wogeo is located, this kind of sorcery is so common—or is alleged to be
—that the residents have coined a term in pidgin English for it, *sangguma*.

technique aimed at bringing about death after sickness can sometimes lead instead to a fatal accident. I drew attention to the
discrepancy, but the reply was always some such remark as,
"Well, there it is; the sorcerer wants the person to die; he doesn't
mind about the means." Even the most articulate of my companions could offer nothing further.

First, over a period of days or weeks the sorcerer watches his
intended victim to learn something of his (or her) habits so that
there will be a reasonable chance of coming upon him alone. Then
he arms himself with a needle-like sliver of black palmwood or a
length of sharp stingray spine and the appropriate "medicines,"
and he collects a couple of assistants who have been warned to
hold themselves in readiness. All go off to the spot where the
victim is likely to be. The assistants at once take him (or her) from
behind and blindfold him with a strip of barkcloth. The sorcerer
thereupon emerges from the bushes and recites a spell that has the
effect of rendering the person unconscious. He falls backwards on
the ground with eyes rolled upwards beyond the lids; but he still
breathes, and his heart continues beating. The sorcerer then
removes the clothing from the prostrate body and places it on the
ground behind. Next the assistants hammer the neck, shoulders,
chest, back, and legs with a stone till these are black with bruises.
They move to one side, and again the sorcerer takes over. He
drives his needle into the person's left side under the ribs; or he
may push it into the anus or urethra; and he may even remove
some vital organ, such as a lung or kidney, and replace it with a
stone, earth, or leaves. He also cuts the ligament under the tongue.
Any blood he wipes away before rubbing the wounds with bespelled "medicines," an action that causes them to close up or
disappear—not a single cut is visible, not a single bruise. Finally,
standing behind the victim, he places other "medicines" on the
eyes and mouth and recites further spells to restore him to life and
destroy all memory of what has taken place. Sorcerer and assistants then hide behind bushes. If the victim, however dizzy, goes
straight to the pile of clothing and replaces the garments the
sorcery is working—he will attend to the day's tasks as usual and
probably make plans for the future. But if he is so ill as to be
indifferent to his nakedness, this means that he is aware of having

been bewitched and of the identity of his assailants. Then the whole process has to be repeated.

Sorcerer and assistants, fully satisfied that from their point of view all is well and that they have not been recognized, proceed to a mountain pool to bathe in the fresh water and wash away the spirit of the person they have harmed. When clean they smear one armpit with charcoal, stamp the foot, and turn in a circle. Here is the first disagreement. Some people maintain that the conspirators select the left armpit and left foot and turn in an counterclockwise direction, just like anyone else who has been in contact with the supernatural; others are positive that with this *yabou* sorcery, because it is aimed at causing death, the opposite is called for— the right armpit, right foot, and a clockwise turn. This latter view seems to me to be illogical, though probably the question is of no more than academic interest. As I shall indicate presently, there is not much likelihood of such sorcery's ever being performed. Yet the evidence is clear that it is regarded as something out of the ordinary.

The victim completes his (or her) work, but that night begins to feel ill. His throat is sore, his limbs ache from the battering, and, according to where the needle has been lodged, he feels acute pain. He and the members of the household think first of disease sorcery and accordingly resort to magic. Or, if a male patient has not menstruated lately, his relatives advise him to perform the *sara* operation forthwith. But in fact for *yabou* there is no remedy, and inevitably he grows weaker and weaker. At the same time, because he has no recollection of the handling he received, he will deny that anything untoward has taken place. Even if by a miracle he should remember, the severing of the tongue ligament would prevent his naming the sorcerer. All too soon he dies.

Some men advanced the theory that after death the wounds open and the end of the palmwood or stingray spine can be detected. This theory others deny. Plenty of people have died as a result of *yabou*, they say, but who, with his own eyes, has ever seen a wound on the corpse? No, this theory is an old woman's story not to be taken seriously by those with experience. Curiously, I found no record of an autopsy. Perhaps the conviction that the needle is employed is so firmly entrenched that a search for objective proof is unnecessary.

Further differences of opinion are expressed over how the spe-
cialized knowledge of spells and "medicines" is transmitted.
Those who follow the conventional line and argue that the sorcerer stresses the left-hand side say that these secrets are like any
other wealth and go to the sons or brothers' sons—though they
admit that, despite the fact that women are debarred from em-
ploying the magic, an aunt or a sister can act as a trustee for a
minor. Those who elect for the right hand, however, argue for
inheritance by the sisters' sons, partly because anything so harmful ought to be treated in a special way, partly because ownership
is supposed to carry risks. A sorcerer is always in danger of vengeance being taken against him, and, in addition, the rites themselves can kill him if he does not perform them regularly. Nobody
likes to think that he might be responsible, even indirectly, for the
death of his own offspring.

The sorcerer selects his potential pupils by preparing in their
presence a potion made from pounded scorpions, centipedes, hor-
nets, and ants. Those who are revolted and decline to drink are
barred from the instruction. But to those who finish the cup
without flinching he teaches the spells and the preparation of the
"medicines." Then, as a test, he has them kill, in order, a rat, a dog,
a pig, a child, and an adult. The kinship relationship of the last two
is not specified, and he advises the selection of persons least likely
to be missed, such as cripples and good-for-nothings. Novices who
are successful in the examination he salutes as fully qualified. Yet
further ritual is called for after the first spontaneous kill. When the
victim has been buried, the operator must thrust a spear into the
grave, push a fine bamboo down the hole, and suck up a quantity
of blood from the corpse. The mourners set a close watch, and the
job is thus highly dangerous. Often it is achieved with the aid of
a spell of invisibility learned from the teacher. Then, during the
next thunderstorm, the new sorcerer climbs to the mountain top
"with his arms outstretched like the wings of a bird of prey" and
there gives three squawking cries. Later he bathes in fresh water,
passes a stone round his head and throws it away, stamps his foot,
and turns round. As before there are schools of thought about
whether he works with his left hand or his right.

As assistants the sorcerer normally chooses his heirs—sons and
brothers' sons according to some, sisters' sons according to others.

But sometimes two or three sorcerers enter into a reciprocal arrangement to give help on request; and occasionally a sorcerer depends on his blood brother.

People take precautions against sorcery automatically, and, more out of habit than ever present fear, they endeavor to find a companion when making a journey or working in the cultivations. At such times, too, they like to have the family dog at their side to give a warning of approaching strangers. Only after a death has occurred do they become noticeably afraid. For a few weeks they cancel any arrangements to visit kinsfolk resident elsewhere, garden in groups of half a dozen, and bar the door at nightfall. But normality soon returns, and after a couple of months talk of the black arts is seldom heard.

It should be noted that the Wogeo, unlike some other Melanesians, do not rely on water or fire for protection. They were incredulous when I told them that the people of Guadalcanal had assured me I would always be safe from sorcerers if I remembered to walk on the beach or alongside a stream. If threatened, these natives had said, all I need do was to wet my hands and feet—the chill of the water would neutralize the sorcery. In both Wogeo and Guadalcanal, however, it is thought that if a sorcerer bespells a woman and then has intercourse with her during the state of trance he will immediately lose his powers.

The Performance of Sorcery

The question that immediately springs to mind is whether this form of death sorcery is ever practiced. Clearly in the literal sense it cannot be. There is no possibility of the instant removal of the marks of cuts or of bruises nor of anyone's surviving the removal of a vital organ. I would also rule out the employment of hypnosis. A rare individual may be capable of being forced by suggestion to surrender his will to live, but an attempt to apply the methods to a normal person would lead to instant discovery. Yet there is still a chance that some men may genuinely believe themselves to be sorcerers. If so they must rely not on reality but on controlled dreaming to carry out their nefarious practices.

I have said that several of my companions were able to list the sorcerers and that the names were commonly those of men resident in other districts. The vast majority were headmen, and the inhabitants of each place enumerated leaders from every district except their own. Thus the Wonevaro pointed to the headmen of Bagiau, Ga, Bukdi, and Takul; whereas the Bagiau omitted the local headmen but added those from Wonevaro. It seems that an accusation, never voiced when the man or his close kinsmen are present, is a mark of his eminence. The fact of his being influential makes him a target for suspicion.

Marigum, the outstanding headman on the island, appeared in the catalogue furnished by all my informants living outside Wonevaro. People were afraid to cross him, I was told, because if he became angry with you he could so easily cause your death. But the Wonevaro residents, when I enquired of them if the charge was well-founded, always denied it. He was too big and valued his reputation too highly to stoop to underhanded methods of punishment or vengeance, they maintained. Like all great men, he acted openly and never hesitated in condemning to their face those who displeased him.

This view was confirmed by Marigum's public reaction when the Falala villagers accused his favorite son Dal of destroying their crops with magic.[3] At the subsequent general meeting to investigate the matter, he expressed the strongest resentment at the fact that anyone imagined that a member of his family would resort to such a mean trick. "We work not with crooked spells but with straight spears," he stormed. As it turned out, Dal's innocence was established beyond doubt by my supplying an alibi. At the time that the sorcery was alleged to have been performed he was helping me develop photographic films. But when later I suggested in private that he be taught the magic to blast growing taro and sent to ruin the gardens of the Falala villagers in revenge for their slander, Marigum was overjoyed. He acted at once and, as I had hoped, taught me the spells as well. One conclusion is obvious—that the talk of being above the use of sorcery is not to be taken seriously. But it is also reasonable to suppose that the suspicion of being familiar with the black arts is not unwelcome. Here is proof

[3] I. Hogbin, "The Father Chooses His Heir," *Oceania*, Vol. II (1940-1941), pp. 37-39.

to the man about whom the gossip is circulating that he is indeed socially significant; moreover, he is assured that his words will be listened to with attention.

The Inquest

Firsthand accounts of inquests are almost as difficult to come by as those of sorcery itself. Certainly a small number of men know what to do, but although they admit the fact openly, attendance at an inquest is restricted to a handful of seniors. All the experts are headmen. This means that the final say as to whether a death is to be avenged, and if so by what means, rests by right with the community leaders. At the same time, full account must be taken of public opinion. A decision without popular support could not be implemented.

No inquests were performed during my stay on the island, and I had to rely on two full descriptions—which were in essentials identical—one from Marigum, the other from a headman of Gol village, and the comments of some half a dozen other men who had at different times witnessed the proceedings. There are two methods, known respectively as *sua maratigi* ("to ask the bamboo") and *yiwo maratigi* ("to ask the spear"). All the specialists are familiar with both, but some prefer one and some the other. In the former the man takes a feather that has formed part of the decorations of the corpse, a stone from the grave, and a Cordyline leaf; he rubs them on the floor of the house where the body lies exposed and stuffs them into a length of bamboo, which he plugs with a leaf stopper. The occupants then leave the building, and he closes the door. One end of the bamboo he pushes through a hole in the wall, and he allows the other to rest on the membrane of a drum placed ready on the ground. Next he recites a spell to conjure up the ghost. On its arrival he tells it to enter the house and grasp the end of the bamboo and by this means to reveal whether sorcery has been carried out. Finally the bamboo is bespelled and rubbed with "medicines." He then places his hand lightly upon it and, in a low whisper, asks a series of questions, all of them so phrased that the answer is a plain yes or no. "Did you die from *yabou* sorcery?" "Whence did the sorcerer come—from the north?" "From the south?" "Was he from Such-and-such a district?" "Was he from X village?" For "no" the bamboo remains steady, for "yes" it shakes the expert's hand and so taps on the drum. Afterwards he dismisses the ghost and throws the bamboo and its contents into the sacred area behind the clubhouse.

Informants assured me that the specialists do not put names before the ghost for it to indicate once and for all who the killer was. There is no need to do so. If the settlement is revealed, they said, to pick the sorcerer is easy.

The other method demands three spears, which have to be fastened together in a frame shaped like the letter H, and a bone of one of the expert's ancestors. This bone is tied to the crosspiece. He rubs the frame with "medicines" and conjures the ghost into it. Then he requests the help of four of the bystanders and has each one rest an end of the frame on an upturned wrist. He himself grasps the bone and crosspiece. The same kind of questions are posed as in the other method, and for the "yes" answer the frame swings downwards on one side.

Obviously with both methods manipulation is simple. Marigum denied absolutely, however, that he or any other expert could be guilty of fraud. An observer would think that bamboo and frame were moving spontaneously, he explained, but this only because the ghost—which, of course, is invisible—has taken control. Whether he believed what he was saying I have no means of telling; but, again, there is nothing exceptional in a medium's unconscious self-delusion.

The majority of other folk accept the disclosure as true, but I found a few sceptics, including my friend Jaua. He had been present at an inquest on three different occasions and once had been asked to take an end of the frame. There was no doubt that it had swung to one side, he agreed; but he was positive the expert must have given it a nudge. He had not seen anything suspicious —but then this is never possible. He went on to say, a fact that Marigum had forgotten to mention, that all inquests take place at night and that lights are not permitted for fear of frightening the ghost; further, the expert speaks so softly that what he says is inaudible, and the people present are in consequence in no position to argue about the verdict. Jaua accepted the reality of sorcery without hesitation, but his interpretation of the inquest was that the man in charge, like most other villagers, makes a guess beforehand as to who the culprit might be and then puts on a theatrical show as a way of magnifying renown and winning extra prestige.

Before Death

We can now pass on to consider the events leading up to the funeral.

Cognates and affines make frequent visits when anyone is ill and may remain chatting for a long period. Those resident nearby send daily gifts of coconuts, choice fruit, and special puddings; if they come from farther afield they arrive with parcels of tobacco, areca nuts, almonds, or dried fish. The members of the stricken family, despite the interference with normal routine, are thus able to offer suitable hospitality.

As the sickness grows worse, so the callers appear more often, now with their older children. They hesitate to raise the subject of death, but if the patient introduces it they do not feel compelled to brush his remarks aside or to encourage him with assurances that he will before long be on his feet again. "Soon I must take the path that everyone will be called on to travel," murmured one old villager to his weeping descendants. "My parents are along the way, and perhaps tomorrow I'll be seeing them." "No, no, no, our father, don't leave us yet," begged a daughter. "To be buried is something we have to face," he replied. "True, true," one of the sons confirmed, "but we'll be here at your side till you go."

Usually, at this point the dying person makes final dispositions and utters any last requests. As a rule, a man will have indicated to his children long before which plots each is to receive as an inheritance, but one who has omitted to do so now gives the appropriate instructions. Some men and women ask to be carried in a litter along the forest tracks so that they may bid farewell to the different areas where they were wont to till the soil, and it is not unknown for them to request burial at the edge of a garden rather than in the settlement. Invariably the relatives agree, though when the time comes they do not always honor the promise.

As soon as it is obvious that the moment of dissolution is fast approaching, the nearer relatives assemble in the house. Several of my friends said that a brother or a son might produce the family store of valuable ornaments in order to frighten the dying individual into prolonging the struggle. They explained that if he could only be made to grasp that these things were ready for decorating his body, the terrifying thought would impel him to further effort. But they denied ever witnessing so macabre a display, and perhaps really such incidents do not occur.

At the last breath the members of the company utter piercing shrieks, and one of them goes outside and tolls the death signal on the slit gong. The beat varies according to the person's age and sex, and identification is therefore easy—provided, of course, that the hearers are aware of the circumstances. All the settlements within earshot repeat the message, thus allowing the more distant kin to start preparations immediately. It is their job to transmit the news by word of mouth to the residents of other districts.

Beating the wooden slit-gong to send a message.

The Ceremonies

The status of the deceased serves to determine how elaborate the ceremonies are to be, how long they are to continue, and how many are to attend. For a young child only members of the immediate family and their closest kin are present, and they return to work after a few days. On the other hand, when a headman has died practically the entire island population comes along, and often the affairs of the village to which he belonged are upset for a period of months. My description will be based on the funeral of a householder of reasonable standing, though I shall indicate a few of the possible variations.

The chief mourners should be the closest relatives—for a young person the parents, the uncles and aunts, and the grandparents; and for an adult the spouse, the children, the brothers and sisters, and the nephews and nieces. Anyone else may wail, but these folk are obliged to do so. Theirs also is the responsibility for making the corpse ready for burial, though, again, other relatives are free to help. Contact with a dead body renders the living taboo, however, and certain restrictions have to be observed. If the deceased had been someone of note in the community, the obligations are accepted without question, but people feel that the loss of an ordinary householder, or of a woman (unless she was the wife of a headman), scarcely justifies a large number of individuals being put to inconvenience. The parents and the spouse are never exempt, but often one relative does duty for all in the same class as himself—a single uncle for the uncles and aunts in general, for instance, or a single brother or a sister for the siblings in general. The selection depends on such considerations as who volunteers from motives of deep affection, who acted at the last funeral, and who has the fewest young children to care for.

The restrictions are similar to those with which we are already familiar—a prohibition on touching the skin with the fingers or fingernails and total abstinence to begin with, followed by the use of a fork when eating, of a straw when drinking, and of a cigarette holder when smoking. At the same time, the ritual coldness associated with mourning is held to be more intense than is customary in the taboo condition, and in consequence greater emphasis is placed on the measures necessary to restore the patient's normal temperature.

Mourners are referred to by the term for spirits of the dead, *mariap*. People deny that such folk are actually ghosts but maintain that association with the deceased leads to a resemblance.

The first task is washing the corpse with hot water. If it is that of a man the mourners shave the beard and forehead, and if it is that of a woman who has left a young child they tie a skirt or a bundle of fibers in the arms to comfort the ghost, which is supposed to be hoodwinked into thinking that the baby also has died. They then dress the body in new clothing and lay it on a fresh palm spathe, referred to as "the canoe of death." They oil the hair, dye it red, and, for a man, drag it back through a newly woven wicker cone stitched over with dogs' teeth. Other ornaments include bird-of-paradise skins, rattan armbands, shell armlets, and breast straps embroidered with small shell rings or cowries. Red Cordyline leaves rest on the trunk and sprigs of aromatic herbs along the limbs.

Then the mourners attend to themselves. The parents, widower, or widow rub oil and soot into the scalp, and the others don a cap of twisted palm spathe (sometimes sons and daughters refuse this protection, thereby publicly proclaiming a devotion so intense as to make them indifferent to baldness and grey hairs). All then smear the face and the chest with ashes. For the rest of the day and during the night—that is to say, until the burial—they give themselves up to demonstrations of sorrow. They embrace the feet and legs of the body, call upon the ancestral spirits to welcome the newcomer to the afterworld, and generally lament their bereavement with intermittent wailing and hiccoughing sobs.

Meantime the other householders of the residential cluster—all of whom are, of course, related to the deceased—are required to show anger at being deprived of his companionship. With this end in view they make for his gardens and there seize a number of the taro plants, which they fling on the roof of his house. Afterwards, however, they enter to add their family ornaments to those already arranged on and around the corpse. Any man who feels the death acutely on account of close personal attachment joins in the

wailing for a short period, but the majority retire to the verandah
or some convenient spot nearby. The women follow and usually
make more of a display with their tears, though soon they too step
outside and form small groups. The youths also have a duty to
perform. They are expected to gather piles of green coconuts,
areca nuts, and betel pepper for the refreshment of the sympathiz-
ers who will come to spend the night.

The relatives from the other side of the village and neighboring
settlements start arriving an hour or so before sunset. If the dead
person was not of exalted status, they come along informally in
small parties of about a dozen, the men bearing their ornaments
in a bundle and also a package of herbs. They lay these packages
over the corpse, unless by now it is fully covered, in which case
they take a piece of string and tie them to the rafters overhead.
A few may weep, but both men and women quickly link up with
the local residents and in lowered voices carry on ordinary conver-
sations.

If, on the other hand, the deceased had been a notability, the
residents of each village march in as a separate unified body.
Indeed, for a headman they are preceded by a series of advance
parties of flute players, at whose approach the seated women
gather the children together and flee indoors, there to remain
until the music has ceased some thirty or forty minutes later.

The members of the different groups are present to demonstrate their sense of bereavement, but they also, like the kin from
the village, are under an obligation to express annoyance at the
man's lack of consideration for the living. They express it by
destroying any of his accessible property, such as pigs, dogs,
canoes, and coconut palms. These items form part of the estate,
and the heirs are thus the real losers. In the heat of the moment,
and at times with calculated malice, the marauders may go
beyond what is considered right and smash goods or kill animals
belonging to another villager. After the death of a leader the
wisest course for his followers is therefore to take the precaution
of quickly shifting their movables and livestock to the temporary
care of relatives living elsewhere. Sufferers must never show resentment; they can only wait until a death occurs in the settlement of the culprits and pay them back in kind.

While throughout the night the mourners inside the house wail and embrace the corpse, the relatives outside spend the time singing, often to the accompaniment of hand drums, or rhythmically humming. There are no proper dirges in Wogeo, no hymns specifically associated with funerals, and almost any tune at all is considered suitable—canoe shanties, dance choruses, religious chants, love songs, and so forth. I have even heard popular European melodies that returned laborers have brought back from plantations.

Etiquette forbids cooking while a corpse lies unburied, and the members of the congregation are obliged to forgo their evening meal. They have to make do with the coconuts and betelnut provided by the village youths.

Burial

Preparations for the burial begin soon after dawn, when one of the elders selects a couple of young men to make the spades for digging the grave. The spades are fashioned in the form of a paddle from a particular kind of timber used for no other purpose. Other men collect a quantity of wild ginger plants.

When all is ready those of the male mourners who belong to the moiety opposite to that of the dead man descend from the house and excavate a hole below, removing some of the floor boards first should this be necessary. One or two of the more distant kin of the appropriate moiety may volunteer to assist, although by doing so they render themselves subject to the full rigor of the mourning taboos. For a man of very high rank other headmen of the right moiety come forward. Such helpers, unless they are already well on in years, twist the customary palm spathe over the head. The grave is seldom more than about thirty inches deep, and if the body is emaciated it may be less.[4]

[4]Nowadays the Administration insists that each village must have a cemetery located at least fifty yards from the dwellings. A high fence gives protection from the pigs, and the graves are marked by Croton shrubs and coral boulders. But they are all fakes. The sole occasion on which a cemetery has been used for its intended purpose was when the death occurred while a government officer was actually patrolling the island. Even then reinterment took place immediately after the danger of discovery had passed.

Burying the dead under the house.—Note the taro plants on the roof and the palm-spathe head-covering of some of the mourners.

The gravediggers now return to the house, remove the ornaments from the corpse, apply paint to the face, arms, hands, and feet, and carry it below, where all the chief mourners embrace it once more and utter their final lamentations. Then the gravediggers tie it in the palm spathe on which it has lain and reverently set it to rest, always with the head pointing in the direction of the rising sun ("up" in native parlance). They shovel the earth back, sprinkle it with pebbles, set a dry coconut on top, and around this rearrange the ornaments.

While the burial is in progress one of the close affines or a cross cousin, again belonging to the opposite moiety, drives the spirit out of the land of the living. Somebody may offer himself for the task, or the elders may make a suggestion. He fills his mouth with ginger and, holding a spear in one hand and a flaming torch in the other, prances through the settlement before and behind the dwellings and around and among the groups of bystanders. First he goes from east to west ("down"), then back again from west to east ("up"). At each step he grimaces horribly, grinds his teeth, flourishes spear and torch, and spits a fine spray of gingery saliva. As he reaches the point from which he started he utters a blood-curdling yell, hurls the weapon after the ghost, and follows this with the torch. The spirit is said to make its way to a headland at the extreme east of the island and thence take flight for the after-world.

Mourning Taboos

At last the mourners are ready to take the first steps towards purification, a process that will occupy them for many days. Each one turns to the left, and they set off for the beach, picking up some of the ginger leaves as they go. The men have the first turn, and the women wait till they come back. All immerse themselves completely and afterwards scrape the water off with the leaves, taking care not to touch the skin with the fingers. Then they smear the forehead, arms, and legs with ashes. The next require-ment is that the men should line up on one side of the grave and the women on the other, both facing outwards, so that an elder can pass in between and drop ginger leaves into their palms, which they hold out behind their backs. These leaves they squeeze thoroughly and drop on the ground. Now the elder kindles a fire and heats a long stick, which he offers each one to bite on. This is followed by his spearing areca nuts and betel pepper beans on a bone and feeding some into every mourner's mouth. An assis-tant places coconut shells full of lime among them, and they start chewing the betel mixture. The lime they scoop up for themselves on the end of a bone. Later the housewives of the village present them with a meal of hot curry, which they eat with a bone as a fork. This is their last food for 24 hours, during which period the consumption of liquids is also forbidden. They now shut them-selves into the house of death.

The villagers are free to go off to their gardens and the visitors to make for home. Most of the women take a taro shoot from the roof of the house to plant as a memorial, though after a few weeks have elapsed they always forget which it is.

The mourners stay indoors all day long, speaking only if absolutely necessary and then in a whisper. At night, should the weather be fine, they descend quietly to sleep at the graveside. In the morning, at daybreak, they walk to the beach and again bathe, as before using ginger leaves as towels. They also replace the smears of ashes. On their return the villagers give them a dish of simple food, perhaps a few roasted taro or some steamed bananas. They eat without speaking and go back indoors. But from now on they are allowed to drink coconut fluid provided they suck it through a straw.

The silence of the first day is repeated, but that night when they come out to sleep some of the neighboring householders keep them company by lying beside the other village graves. The usual morning bath follows and brings the period of the most intensive restrictions to a close. Scratching implements, eating forks, and the other paraphernalia can be discarded and the drinking of water resumed. At the same time, although talking and sitting about outside are permitted, all forms of work are banned, and the relatives still have to provide food. Leftovers must also be destroyed lest the dogs eat them and die.

This state of affairs continues for from a few days to a few months, when the senior of the mourners—the father, eldest brother, or eldest son—signifies that the time has arrived for the terminating ceremony. First he calls on some mature woman, one renowned for her skill, to bleed the company and allow the coldness to escape. Then they throw the head covering into the sea and walk to the nearest stream inland, where they bathe in fresh water, men above, women lower down. If on the way back they have to pass through a village the residents give them food.

The next task is to collect ripe coconuts and herbs and from them to make oil. With this oil they anoint the entire body. From that moment they are ritually cleansed and may resume their ordinary life.

The widow, however, is in a special category; she has to stay in semiseclusion for about a year longer if her husband was a headman. She ties a length of old rope (*rai*) around her neck, wrists, and ankles and wears old skirts of dingy brown fibers. Her hair remains uncut, and at intervals she smears herself with ashes or charcoal. Work is permitted, but she may not sit about, join public gatherings, take part in festivities, or raise her voice. If she is young the dead man's brother, after a decent interval, goes along and cuts the ropes, and his wife presents her with a new skirt. She can then go back to her own kinsmen and from their village accept an offer of marriage. But if she is an elderly woman she may retain the marks of her state for good or remove them when at last she feels she has worn them long enough.

Once clean, the mourners who belong to the dead person's village decorate those who live in other places. Next day the neighbors, whether mourners or not, accompany them to their homes. The mourners themselves carry nothing, but the rest of the party brings baskets of food and bundles of fuel with which to cook it on arrival. Ordinarily vegetables and nuts suffice, most of them collected from the estate of the deceased. But a headman who has taken part is always rewarded with at least one pig and sometimes three or four. The gifts are described as payment for digging the grave.

The relatives of those who have come back home are ready with a welcome and even help the party with the preparations. Later, after the repast has been served, they offer more food as a return donation. If possible this donation includes a few packages of dried fish.

Within the next day or two the chief mourner gathers up the various ornaments and returns them to the owners. He also sets the coconut from the grave to one side. No great attention is paid to it, but if it should put forth a shoot and grow, the resulting palm tree is given the name of the dead, though it is not treated with any marked respect.

At this point a blood brother or, more rarely, a distant relative or affine who feels special gratitude to the deceased for out-of-the-way kindnesses may declare what is called a *rae*. This means that, until the embargo is ritually lifted, he will not take food from the hands of those belonging to the dead person's family, nor will he enter their dwellings. (When a headman takes such action the members of his residential group follow: correspondingly, all the members of the dead person's residential group are affected). He implies no criticism of their care and is merely giving a declaration of his personal involvement.

Marigum declared a *rae* on the death of the wife of Bagasal, the headman of the other Dap housing cluster. She was not only the sister of his own first consort but also "famous as a worker and skilful nurse of the sick." About a year went by, and after consultation the two headmen decided that the interdiction should be brought to an end. The ceremony took place during the first few days of my stay. The householders of Marigum's group cooked sago cakes and bowls of vegetable stew, and those of Bagasal's taro and joints of pork. In the late afternoon, when everyone was ready, Bagasal's brother set down a palm spathe with raised edges and into it emptied the contents of several green coconuts. Marigum's kinsfolk approached and, dipping their fingers in the liquid, rubbed it over their faces and chests, thus washing the taboo away. Normal fraternization was now possible, and the piles of food could be exchanged.

When the deceased had been a mature man with descendants, the further duty of disinterring the jaw and some of the other bones devolves on the chief mourner. He postpones the disinterment until such time as the flesh will have decomposed, after an interval of perhaps three or four years. He takes no precautions beforehand and afterwards is content to wash himself thoroughly and rub his hands with ginger. The relics, now smeared with ochre, he places in a basket for storage on a shelf in the club. They are thought to enhance the efficacy of any magic that the dead man had himself used and passed on. As has been indicated, the sons therefore like to rest their hand upon the container when reciting spells, and for this reason they take it with them when making a trading voyage overseas.

The only bodies treated in a different manner from that described are those of women who die in childbirth and of men slain in battle or murdered (by violence, as distinct from sorcery). As I mentioned, the corpse of such a female is buried in the bush, and the relatives do not go into mourning. Usually the same applies to the corpse of a warrior, though I heard of one case in which a headman insisted that his son, who had been killed in an ambush, be laid to rest beneath the village clubhouse. But even then the funeral ceremonies were omitted. The explanation put forward for such apparent callousness is that those who die suddenly are

so unclean that avoidance by the living is essential; ritual purification of those in contact with the corpse would be of no avail, and
inevitably they would perish.

It remains for brief reference to be made to the maimed rites
for an elderly childless widow who died in Dap during my stay.
She had come from the Bagiau district, but after her husband's
death several years before had elected to remain with his kinsmen.
They built her a small hut and regularly cleared ground for her
to cultivate a garden; but they regarded her as incurably lazy.
Never once, so they said, had she offered to mind the children so
that the mothers could work unencumbered. One morning a
young girl taking along a few roasted taro found that she had died,
possibly during the night, possibly a day or two previously. The
villagers informed her Bagiau relatives, who arrived hours later,
just before dark. Meantime the Dap villagers had laid the body out
on the usual sheet of palm spathe. They were reluctant to undergo
the taboos, nevertheless, and, in order to avoid physical contact
with the corpse, had pushed and prodded it with long sticks. Both
parties, the cognates and the affines, kept watch during the night,
but no one came forward to discharge the functions of a mourner.
The result was a complete absence of weeping, and talk replaced
the customary singing. At dawn a couple of lads dug a shallow
grave just outside. The rest then tied the corpse in the spathe,
though they took every care not to touch it, and thrust it into the
hole. The grave proved to be too short, and much maneuvering
with the sticks took place before the bundle could be fitted in.
After the replacement of the soil everyone went off to bathe and
to rub himself with ginger. Further precautions were not considered necessary, and ordinary work began immediately. Those not
directly concerned said that the whole episode was shameful, but
they reserved most of their criticisms for the dead woman. She
ought to have adopted children, they maintained, or else become
a full working member of one of the village households. Had she
done so there would have been people to bury her properly and
carry out the full mourning ritual.

VIII   Magic

Evans-Pritchard, discussing the Nuer, remarked that as
their religion was theistic, magic of necessity played a negligi-
ble role. "When both fortune and misfortune come from God,
they cannot also come from human powers, whether innate or
learned."[1]

Wogeo presents the complete contrast to this observation.
Here there is neither an omnipotent God nor a pantheon of god-
lings, and dependence and supplication receive no emphasis. Indeed, the spirit beings—whether culture heroes, ghosts, or monsters—scarcely impinge on day-to-day activities. They do not
demand sacrifices or hymns of praise and thanksgiving, and
householders never feel a need for seeking divine blessings or
pleading for divine mercy. Clearly in these circumstances a priest-
hood to serve as an intermediary between men and the other
world would be redundant. What we find instead is the universal
practice of magic. Each person owns a set of rites and is convinced
that by performing them he can bring even his most mundane
desires to fulfilment.

Magical knowledge is looked upon as a form of property and
passes down the generations by the accepted rules of inheritance.
All the sons are entitled to a share, though normally fathers re-
serve the most valued forms for the eldest in the expectation
of his using it for the benefit of his brothers. A son with a
notably retentive memory may also be favored, as well as, occa-

[1]E. E. Evans-Pritchard, *Nuer Religion* (Oxford 1956), pp. 316-317.

sionally, a nephew. As a rule instruction begins when a lad is about fifteen or so. He accompanies his father and watches what takes place. Later the parent gives him a few lessons and next time may allow him, under supervision, to take over. But if the father is elderly and the sons mere children, he appoints a trustee—perhaps their mother, a cousin, or his sister. He imparts the secrets to this individual, who later passes them on. It is reported also that sometimes blood brothers exchange magic.

Magic as Control

Magic has a twofold part to play. First it overcomes ignorance and impotence. When a person wants something urgently he takes all the practical steps open to him. If, notwithstanding, the goal is still out of reach, he falls back on magic to bridge the gap. Thus the Wogeo native is sufficiently experienced to be aware that in preparing a new taro garden he must select an area with the right drainage where the soil is of the appropriate texture and the ground has lain fallow for a certain length of time; and after he has cleared the forest growth he erects a stout fence as protection from marauding pigs. Yet a good harvest is still not guaranteed. Accordingly he has recourse to magic to keep down insect pests and to eradicate plant diseases. And because unseasoned softwoods rapidly decay in the tropical climate, there is a rite to give the fence added strength.

I am not implying that the people themselves sharply differentiate between action based on empirical knowledge and action that we would describe as irrational. At times even an informed outsider would be hard put to decide whether a particular procedure was reasonable or magical, and to those inside the society the distinction might be meaningless. Men often answered my scepticism by arguing that performing a rite to banish insects is no less valid than choosing good soil.

It is a fact, of course, as Nadel pointed out, that because a person's wants are determined by tradition, magic protects him from failures that are failures only because his social order has so ordained. Thus "magic is a tool used in the realization of the fortuitously given social values, not only a weapon in man's eternal fight against fate."[2]

The second application of magic occurs in situations where direct action to attain some end would be inexpedient. A man with a grievance against his neighbors, perhaps because they have failed to repay a debt, is perfectly free to accuse them of default and demand compensation. But he has to bear in mind that if he does so future relations will be imperiled. They may become indignant and refuse to cooperate with him further, thereby causing a serious rift in the small village community. Usually, therefore, as was pointed out above (p. 143), he prefers to seek satisfaction by more subtle means. In public he continues to treat the offenders with customary goodwill while secretly carrying out a ceremony to inflict them with some such minor ailment as a toothache or a gastric upset. When one of them next falls ill he is content to think that this is the punishment due and that he is responsible.

Magic, then, may be described as an agency enabling men to control nature by supernatural means. In Wogeo it is thought to work automatically, and, provided the various details of the ritual are carried out exactly as prescribed, the result is a foregone conclusion. A spokesman summing up one of the many discussions I initiated explained what happens by referring to an axe. "When you want to fell a tree you take this implement, and once you've cut through the base nothing can prevent the trunk from toppling to the ground," he said. "So with the rite—say this and do that, and there's your wish. This is the way the culture heroes decreed things should go." Asked if these heroes came along to do what was required, he replied certainly not—had he not already explained how they disappeared before the first ancestors came on the scene? A further query as to whether the ancestors

[2]S. F. Nadel, "Malinowski on Magic and Religion," in R. Firth (ed.), *Man and Culture* (London 1957), p. 193. Kroeber made the same point. He cited the Yurok and Karok Indians of California, who occupied one of the most favorable natural environments in North America and yet needed the assurance of magic to overcome a host of difficulties that other peoples might have considered imaginary (A. L. Kroeber, *Anthropology* [London 1948], p. 309).

might not take over was greeted with ridicule.

Wogeo is in respect of magic, as in many other respects, typical of the western half of Melanesia. To the east, in the Solomon Islands and the New Hebrides, magic, though equally trust-worthy, is believed to achieve effects at second hand. Instead of the initial rite itself doing the job, magic works through the ances-tors and other spirits. Such beings possess as a permanent attribute a special power, always known by the word *mana* (or a linguistic variant such as *mamanaa* or *nanama*), that they can use for the benefit of mortals. Magic is simply a way of compelling them to direct this power into particular channels. In these areas, if we continue with the earlier analogy, the spirits pick up the axe to chop down the tree, forced into doing so by human magic, which thus would appear to resemble a whip; or, if the metaphor is changed, we can say that in the west men turn on the electricity switch of magic themselves, whereas in the east they have to rely on their servants, the spirits, to do so when ordered.[3]

Another Interpretation

The view of magic put forward in the foregoing section has been ridiculed by Douglas as naive to the point of absurdity. In support of her dismissal of this view she quoted the South African Bushmen laughing at an anthropologist who enquired if they imagined their rain ceremony had caused the following storm, and also the Dinka native whom another anthropologist reported as completing the curative rite for malaria and then urging his patients to attend the clinic if they hoped for a recovery. She assigned a blame for the misconception to Frazer and his disciple Malinowski, the latter of whom was so silly as to treat magic as "a poor man's whisky, used for gaining conviviality and courage against daunting odds."[4] The main purpose of ritual, including magical ritual, she informed us, is to aid in the selection of experi-ence for concentrated attention, and hence to encourage creative performance.

[3]Cf. I. Hogbin, *Experiments in Civilization* (London 1939), pp. 117-121; and *A Guadalcanal Society* (New York 1964), pp. 85-89.
[4]M. Douglas, *Purity and Danger* (London 1966), pp. 58-59.

For an external symbol can mysteriously help in the co-ordination of brain and body . . . The Dinka herdsman hurrying home to supper, knots a bundle of grass at the wayside, a symbol of delay. Thus he expresses outwardly his wish that the cooking may be delayed for his return. The rite holds no magic promise that he will now be in time for supper. He does not dawdle home thinking that the action will itself be effective. He redoubles his haste. His action has not wasted time, for it has sharpened the focus of his attention on his wish to be in time.[5]

This interpretation seems to me little different from Malinowski's assertion that magic in the Trobriands was never an excuse for shoddy workmanship; rather, the practitioner, now confident a supernatural force was on his side, made a greater effort and therefore often was successful. I would also question Douglas's bald statements here and elsewhere in her book about symbols. We need evidence to support the contention that a thing stands for another particular thing and not something that for the people themselves is poles apart.[6] It is surely possible that knotted grass may represent loss of appetite by the cook or her sudden recollection of the time-consuming tasks that have occupied the man during the day.[7] Again, although I cannot speak at first hand of African peoples and their denials of the efficacy of magic, undoubtedly any Melanesian asked why he was performing a rite would instantly name a very specific end, cessation of flood rains perhaps or a cure for headache.

[5] *Ibid.*, pp. 63-64.
[6] Cf. V. W. Turner, *The Drums of Affliction* (Oxford 1968), p. 7. "Observed ritual behaviour . . . may initially be meaningless to the alien investigator, or, worse still, he may think he finds meaning in it by drawing on his own experience, and proceed to totally erroneous interpretations of the rites he sees. Each society's ritual symbols constitute a unique code and each society provides a unique key to that code."
[7] Cf. M. Douglas, "The Social Control of Cognition," *Man* (N.S.), Vol. 3 (1968), p. 396. "A standard rite is a symbolic act which draws its meaning from a cluster of standard symbols . . . The rite imposes order and harmony . . . From the physical to the personal, to the social, to the cosmic, great rituals create unity in experience. They assert hierarchy and order. In doing so, they affirm the value of the symbolic patterning of the universe. Each level of patterning is validated and enriched by association with the rest."

Douglas maintained further that magic and other ritual serve to focus attention by providing a frame, thus enhancing the memory and linking the present with the relevant past.

There are those things we cannot experience without ritual. Events that come in regular sequence acquire a meaning from relation with others in the sequence. Without the full sequence individual elements become lost, imperceivable. For example, the days of the week, with their regular succession, names, and distinctiveness: apart from their practical value in identifying the divisions of time, they have a meaning as part of a pattern. Each day has its own significance and if there are habits which establish the identity of a particular day, these regular observances have the effect of ritual. Sunday is not just a day of rest. It is the day before Monday, and equally for Monday in relation to Tuesday. In the true sense we cannot experience Tuesday if for some reason we have not formally noticed that we have been through Monday. Going through one part of the pattern is a necessary procedure for being aware of the next part. Air travellers find that this applies to hours of the day and the sequence of meals. These are examples of symbols which are received and interpreted without having been intended. If we admit that they condition experience, so we must admit also that intended rituals in regular sequence can have this as one of their important functions.[8]

Further on, with approval Douglas quoted Lienhardt on the regular rain ceremonies of the Dinka. "In these . . . human symbolic action moves with the rhythm of the natural world . . . recreating that rhythm in moral terms . . ."[9]

I am doubtful about the analogy, for when crossing the International Date Line from east to west, thereby losing one day of the week, I at least have never had difficulty in orienting myself; yet with regard to magical ceremonies that are carried out at a certain period each year or in strict order during a given enterprise, such

[8] M. Douglas, *Purity and Danger* (London, 1966), pp. 64-65.
[9] *Ibid.*, p. 66, quoting R. G. Lienhardt, *Divinity and Experience* (London 1961), p. 280.

as the organization of an overseas trading voyage, we can perhaps agree with the general argument. Much of the magic of Wogeo, however, is concerned with events that arise haphazardly. Sorcery is performed only by a man who has been offended, health magic only when someone is ill, fishing magic only if hauls have been poor, magic to calm the wind only during the rages of a tempest, and so on.

Types of Magic

Properly speaking, there is no term in Wogeo for magic as a whole, though occasionally in this context I have heard people using *bwasa*, which ought to be reserved for the spell, the form of words to be recited (like "Open sesame" in the Arabian Nights story of Ali Baba and the Forty Thieves). Instead there is a series of names, one for each of the many kinds of magic. The following are selected at random: *kalingo* (literally "good"), to promote health and cure illness; *ngarul*, to enhance personal appearance, whether from vanity, to outshine rivals, or to attract someone of the opposite sex; *bwasa mau* or *mwanubwa mau* ("spell taro" or *Cordyline terminalis* taro), to increase the fertility of a garden; *muj*, to cause harm to other people or their property, as, for example, by inflicting them with ailments or by inducing pigs to destroy their crops; *kinaba* ("to nod"), to encourage neighbors to refrain from squabbling and live at peace with one another; *dan sauasaua* ("water flowing swiftly"), to ensure easy childbirth; *jala tun* ("road block"), to prolong a woman's labor in revenge for her having spurned the magician's advances; *lala* or *ngies* (two varieties of ginger), to bring good hauls of fish; *yaka mwosmwos* ("pregnant"), to add to a trading partner's good will and hence influence him to be generous; *bwab*, to protect property against theft; *varang* ("sun"), weather magic; *kua*, war magic; and *yabou*, sorcery in which one of the victim's vital organs is removed. Other kinds, all named, include canoe magic, inquest magic, magic to endow a person with skill as a flautist, magic to keep a wife faithful, magic to make pigs fat, magic to reduce a guest's appetite, magic to lengthen the day when people are about to enjoy themselves at a festival—even magic to improve a boy's memory so that he will not forget any detail of his magical inheritance.

We can divide the types of magic into two categories: rites concerned with the welfare of groups of people and rites associated with the affairs of individuals or perhaps the members of a simple family. The former are in the hands of specialists, mostly headmen, and are backed up by myths about some of the more important culture heroes. The Dap magic for overseas trade, for example, has as its source the story of the hero Mafofo's first voyage (pp. 42-48). As was indicated, although everyone in the village is acquainted with the events of the tale in a general way, the details are known solely to the headman, Marigum, whose exclusive property they are. When Marigum organizes a trading expedition the ritual follows point for point the doings of Mafofo. The people say that this myth and the others like it are "the foundation" of the magic, using a word that also means "trunk of a tree," "base," "cause."

Weather magic provides another instance of magic conducted for the welfare of groups. I recorded hearsay evidence of droughts, but they appear to have occurred at long intervals, perhaps twice in a century. Although magic to cause showers exists to cope with such situations, it is rarely used and is not considered to be of outstanding value. The more frequent problem is too much rain, leading to landslides and washed-out gardens. Accordingly, the rites for which a headman is so highly esteemed are those to banish chilling downpours and call up the life-giving warmth of the sunshine. "The sun makes the gardens flourish," Marigum once told me. "It causes the coconuts to fill out, the taro to swell, and the bananas to ripen." What about the rain? Was it not also essential, I enquired. No, he replied, the cold of the rain hinders growth.

Each of the headmen I knew well had his own weather magic. Marigum's was derived from the culture hero Daru, an emissary of the sun. In the time of the heroes the sun regularly descended from the sky by means of the mythical *malal* tree to visit a Wogeo blood brother, bringing all sorts of rich foodstuffs with it. But after a quarrel the hero in question cut the *malal* down, for which reason the species is no longer found. The sun, enraged, sent the follower Daru down a shorter tree with orders to kill the hero; but it allowed Daru to leave behind on earth the magic to make the rain stop. This magic, in due course, Marigum inherited.

The rites of the Gol headman Janggara came from the heroes Tarelinga and Mandoa. One day when gardening these two cursed the sun for being too hot. Immediately they heard a voice from the sky telling them to look seawards. There they saw a shoal of fish, which, in their excitement they followed in a canoe until the land had disappeared below the horizon. Eventually they drifted to another island, where a headman of extraordinary beauty received them. He told them to collect coconuts. At first these were no bigger than an almond, but as soon as the headman touched them they began to grow larger. The same kind of thing happened to taro and bananas. The headman then explained that he was really the sun and had been annoyed at their cursing him. But once they had expressed their regrets he sent them back to Wogeo with weather magic as a parting gift.

The second category of rites, those with a narrower purpose, are occasionally enshrined in myths, but as a rule where this is so the stories are of purely local interest. If there is no such reference to a myth, the owner fortifies his trust with instances of past fantastic successes—of fishing magic that so rewarded a grandfather that tuna became available for every resident in the entire district, of fertility magic that caused a sow to produce a litter of twenty piglets, of misfortune magic that led to no less than ten poisonous snakes entering an enemy's dwelling in the course of a single night, and so forth.

Analysis of Magic

Generally magic has three elements—the spell or verbal formula, the substance transmitting the special power from the magician to the persons or objects to be influenced, and the set actions he has to perform.

In theory spells are repeated without the slightest alteration, and the wording remains absolutely constant. Certainly a man makes every endeavor to teach his heirs correctly, and they in turn take pains to follow him syllable by syllable; but doubtless memories sometimes play tricks. Yet it should be noted that many expressions are archaic—or are said to be archaic—and that sometimes the practitioner, while able to convey the sense of what he is saying, cannot give a literal phrase-by-phrase translation into contemporary idiom. I also found that over and over again when two spells were identical they seemed to have been derived from a single source, perhaps a grandfather or great-grandfather common to both the present owners.

There are exceptions, but the specialist spells—those relating to group concerns—tend to be short, often no more than four or five words taken straight from the myth. I shall be quoting other examples later, but for the present it will suffice to give the spell of a Dap headman to ensure that a new trading canoe, traditionally always called *Urem Tariga* (see p. 43), will make directly for the intended destination and not drift with the current. He takes soft leaves and, rubbing the figurehead with a gentle motion, murmurs simply, "Jina, your eyes are clear, your eyes are bright." This is a reference to the myth of the blind woman whose sight was restored (p. 36.)

The other spells are longer, and some might run the full length of a printed page. All are in rhythmical language and are thus not only easier to learn than a passage of prose but also a great deal easier to remember. They speak of the desired aim as if it had already been achieved and are full of figures of speech and far-fetched analogies. A spell to produce a prolific crop, for example, may well compare the taro plants with huge Ficus trees and the corms with boulders too heavy to lift; one to make a canoe sail swiftly may apostrophize it as faster than the flight of an eagle; one to improve a dancer's appearance may tell of his well-oiled skin as smooth as a water-worn pebble and of his eyes bright as the full moon; and one to intensify a warrior's ferocity may liken him to a crocodile or venomous snake. It might, indeed, be argued that magical spells offer some clue to the origin of poetry.

If the spell is backed by a myth, the name of the culture hero is mentioned, and often at the end there is a list of the ancestors reputed to have owned the magic in times gone by. A few men suggested that calling the names was in a sense a summons to the spirits—if present they would silently correct any verbal mistake and therefore make success doubly certain—but the majority insisted that this was a misinterpretation. The heroes had disappeared for good, my more knowledgeable associates pointed out again; and once dead an ancestor is without influence. The orthodox view is that the sole object of telling over these earlier practitioners is to give present reassurance. You remind yourself that the magic would never have been handed down through so many generations were it not efficacious. This explanation is in line with that offered for a magician wanting to hold the skeletal relics of his forebears while performing an important rite (p. 166). The bones comfort him by bringing before his eyes the persons who in his youth had cared for him and given him protection. All was well then, and now he feels that all will be well in the future.

The second element in magic is the medium for its transmission. This we may refer to as the "medicine." The magician recites or chants his spell over it and proceeds to bring it into contact with whatever he wishes to dominate or alter. In garden magic he buries the "medicine" in the center of the plot or at one of the corners; in canoe magic he rubs it over the dugout or fastens it to an outrigger boom; in beauty magic he wipes it on the man's body or thrusts it into his armlets; in fighting magic he heats it in a cooking pot and sprinkles the liquid over the warriors; in magic to lengthen the hours of daylight he scatters it at dawn in the direction in which the sun will rise; and in magic to cause illness he places it in the victim's bed or just outside the house so that the man is bound to step on it.

Selection of the "medicine," as with the phrasing of the spell, is determined by superficial analogies. That for gardening consists of leaves or bark cut from very tall trees or trees bearing large fruits (these may or may not be edible); that for increasing the speed of a canoe, of feathers of birds well known as swift in flight; that for beauty, of brightly colored flowers or sweet-smelling herbs; that for warlike prowess, of dried snake crushed to powder or scrapings from a stick picked up near a grave; that for a longer day, of lime or white dust filed from the surface of a lump of coral;

Magic to keep the outrigger float of a canoe firmly attached to the booms.

that for illness, of various unpleasant substances such as thorns, stinging nettles, the excrement of pigs, or fragments of a plant with an evil-smelling flower.

In most types of health magic the magician has to pound the "medicine" to pulp, place it in a container, and fill the vessel with coconut fluid or water. He mixes the ingredients together and orders the patient to drink the concoction. Such a potion is called a *karag*. The majority of them appear to have no effect, but a small number act as a purge. On one or two occasions when someone was ill I watched a *karag* being brewed without the recitation of a preliminary spell. On my expressing astonishment, the doctor always insisted that in this instance the "medicine" was by itself sufficient. Other people agreed with the statement and added that this was the only kind of magic lacking a form of words. It is still possible, however, that through the years the spell had been forgotten.

We now come to the third element, the magician's actions.

Some of the specialist spells, owned by leaders, are by tradition chanted aloud, and those standing nearby have no difficulty in overhearing. Yet they would not dream of stealing this sort of magic for themselves. They look upon it as a private possession of their social superiors, who have inherited the knowledge by right of birth. Ordinary people, on the other hand, take precautions against theft. They whisper their spells or hum them over so softly as to be barely audible.

The initial step is chewing a mouthful of ginger "to make the words hot"—that is, to augment their potency. The magician then holds the "medicine" close to his mouth, clasping it tightly by way of concealment. At the end of each line of the spell he breathes upon it or blows a fine spray of ginger-impregnated saliva all over it.

This practice of puffing and spitting is common throughout the western Pacific, though each society seems to have an explanation peculiar to itself. The Wogeo view depends upon the prevailing physiological theories. The people maintain that breath is necessary for life, just as petrol is necessary to make a motor work. Sucked in through the nose and mouth, it passes to the lungs (*buso*) for storage. The lungs therefore contain the body's fuel tanks and hence are the most important of the organs. They pass breath on to the heart to enable it to pump the vital heat from the trunk to the head, arms, and legs. The throbbing can be felt through all the arteries and veins (a distinction the natives ignore) in the same way as the engine vibrations lead to the whole car quivering. But the lungs hold more than air: To them also go the impressions absorbed through the eyes and ears. Thus they are the repository of memory, the center of thought, and the seat of emotion.[10] Obviously a man keeps his magic there, and when using it he has to blow or spit to expel the last shred.

Some forms of magic, but by no means all of them, call for miming on the part of the practitioner. In magic to keep villagers at peace with one another he bows his head first to the right and then to the left as though greeting an acquaintance (hence the name *kinaba*, "to nod"). In magic to make warriors fierce and hence victorious in battle he grimaces with assumed rage. In that to cause serious illness he stabs with an imaginary spear, and in that to calm the wind during a gale he performs the gestures of pacifying a child's temper tantrums.

Malinowski, writing of magic in the Trobriand Islands, spoke of a fourth element—the condition of the performer, who there was frequently obliged to prepare himself, or protect himself afterwards, with rituals. We have seen that in Wogeo there are specific requirements for the types of magic regarded as of particular significance, such as that associated with the formal nomination of the heir by a headman. The person is set apart, taboo, *rekareka*, and in consequence must first fast for a period and later must eat with a fork and drink through a straw. The demands of other magic are less rigorous. Most men think it advisable to refrain from sexual intercourse and from eating nuts for a full twenty-four hours if they are expecting to perform gardening or fishing magic, but a few dismiss such behavior as superstition. Their attitude resembles that of those Europeans who scorn touching wood after boasting of good luck, throwing salt over the left shoulder when some has been spilled, and avoiding walking under a ladder.

Examples

I shall begin with one or two of the specialist rites.

When a feast is held, the headman has the duty of performing

---

[10]There are separate words for the different emotions of joy, sorrow, anger, and fear; but the last two are often grouped together and referred to as *ilo* (or *iloilo*) *ereka*, literally "inside bad."

the magic to preserve peace and harmony. I watched the ceremony in Gol village, and afterwards the officiating leader taught me what to do. First I must take ginger root and the leaves from two lianas, the *waluo* and the *dabara*, and chew them all together. Then, just before the food distribution, I should stand firmly with my feet apart "like an immovable rock" and chant the following spell over the assembled people:

> "The tree standing tall,
> Fastened securely, covered entirely,
> With *waluo* and *dabara* vines.
> My beloved village,
> Fastened securely, covered entirely,
> With *waluo* and *dabara* vines.
> Old baskets are black,
> Black over the hearth,
> Blackened by the smoke.
> Food to eat, much food,
> Fastened, secure, held tightly."

At the end of each line I must spit some of the contents of my mouth over the folk on my left, then over those on my right, with a polite nod, *kinaba*. From that moment quarreling would cease.

This man showed me how the *waluo* and *dabara* lianas cover a tree so completely that the branches are locked in and do not rub against one another. The tree thus resists the force of the strongest winds and remains firm. Further, the thorny tangle is so thick that nobody can approach to take the fruit or wield an axe. The magic has the effect of giving the settlement the same stability. The different families do not rub against one another, outside groups are prevented from overthrowing them, and sorcerers fear to carry out their evil designs. The old baskets are a sign of peace —they have remained undisturbed in the smoke for so long.

The headman also carries out beauty magic over his followers before they hold a dance or embark on an overseas voyage. When Marigum performs he chews ginger and holds a branch of scarlet hibiscus flowers and crimson Cordyline leaves. He walks along the line of men chanting:

"Mafofo grew tall; my kinsmen and I grow tall.
Mafofo was upright; my kinsmen and I are upright.
Mafofo washed and anointed himself with oil;
My kinsmen and I wash and anoint ourselves with oil.
Our skin is smooth, smooth as white clamshell.
The stranger stood amazed
And then ran forwards to gape at Mafofo.
The strangers will run forwards to gape at my kinsmen
     and me."

He also spits over the crowd and touches each person lightly with the bunch of red flowers and leaves.

For a trading excursion a second rite is necessary to influence the various partners. Marigum's spell runs, "Mafofo's partner's foot itched: then the man gave good things." An itching foot is a sign that somebody is talking about you. The partner is thus warned of the magic to make him generous and that he will be powerless to resist.

An anomalous form of beauty magic may be mentioned here. In this there is no one practitioner, and the members of the dancing or trading party assemble in the clubhouse to sing songs that have miraculous overtones. Each man brings brightly coloured flowers or sweet-smelling herbs and fastens them to the rafters over his head. The performances may last all night, with the usual hand-drum and slit-gong accompaniment. The songs refer to the culture heroes. As a rule there are only about half a dozen words, but these are repeated in endless permutations and combinations. A typical specimen runs, "the doves in a tree billing and cooing," an allusion to one of the myths of the origin of marriage. Kamarong, the bridegroom, was ignorant of how to express his admiration for his bride, Jari, and accordingly took the birds as his model (p. 35). In the morning the men carry away their decorations, now endowed with the power to attract boundless admiration to the wearer. These they set aside till the time comes for fixing them in their armbands. They retain them to the end but add fresh specimens daily.

The rite to attract the affections of a young girl will serve as an initial example of private magic. I learned of it from my cook (by

Love magic.

a coincidence appropriately named Gris), then aged about seventeen or eighteen. He gathered a quantity of heavily scented white flowers from *sibula* and *juju* bushes and out of them wove a garland for his hair, a chain for his neck, and a belt for his waist. Then he picked up a bamboo whistle, ordinarily used when a suitor wishes to serenade the person of his choice, and retired to a quiet corner. The spell was short:

> "Kamarong took two *sibula* flowers,
> Scented *sibula* flowers.
> The *juju* flowers open,
> Jari sees the flowers open."

Instead of spitting or breathing heavily at the line endings he blew a few notes on the whistle, the noise of which was to act as the "medicine" and carry the magic to the girl's ears and hence to her understanding.

One more example will be enough. I shall take the magic with which my friend Jaua protected his groves of areca nuts and orchards from theft. After he had performed it any person who stole nuts or fruit ran the risk of contracting the loathsome disease gangosa, which begins with a sore on the face and ends with the nose entirely eaten away.

Jaua picked up his "medicines" and recited this spell over them:

> "Oh Noabahagi! [the hero who first used the magic]
> Oh fish-hawk!
> Your claws are sharp, your teeth are sharp;
> Eat the thief's face.
> I place you on the leaves beneath the palms.
> Eat the face of him who steals and make many holes in it.
> He lies sleepless, he howls at night [at this point Jaua himself
>   howled],
> He weeps at night;
> Morning comes, and he still cannot sleep.
> Your claws dig in! Tear away!
> I place you on the road. Watch well.
> A thief steals my things.
> They are not his but mine.
> Eat blood, eat skin, eat nose.

The centipedes bite, the black ants bite,
The fish-hawk tears, the stingray stings.
Eat his face."

As he spoke, he made the gestures of a hawk tearing its prey to pieces. At the end he spat on the leaves and tied them to a tree as a warning.

Magic to render this first rite ineffective is essential before the owner of the grove collects his property. He fashions a tiny broom from dried grass and sweeps the palm trunks while uttering a spell to send the fish-hawk into the clouds, the centipedes and ants to a mountain cave, and the stingrays to a distant reef. Then, after he has satisfied his needs, he reimposes the ban.

As is usual, magic to cause a disease goes hand in hand with magic to cure it. The spell to relieve gangosa is as follows:

> "Oh Yap! Oh Rog! [two heroes from Manam Island, an
>   active volcano]
> The sore is dry.
> The sore is above Manam,
> The sore is above Bam [another active volcano: the great
>   heat is expected to dry up the sore].
> It is dry, dry as tinder;
> It is smooth, smooth bark.
> Oh Kuakua! [a hero who survived in battle by drinking the
>   blood from his wounds]
> Suck up the blood and carry it away to the tall *tora* tree
>   [so that the patient's head will feel light once more].
> Nose smooth, sores away;
> Cheeks smooth, sores away;
> Lips smooth, sores away."

The magician on reaching the last line utters a sucking noise as though he were removing the pus and blood.

Infallibility of Magic

When talking about magic in a general way, people always stress that it can be depended upon implicitly. As I said, they insist

that it cannot fail and in confirmation are prepared to cite successes by the hundred. So convinced are they of its reliability that
a simple explanation is ever ready at hand when they are con-
fronted with a particular instance of results falling short of what
had been expected. The magician must have made a mistake in
the spell—perhaps he inadvertently left out some of the words,
interpolated extra expressions, or quoted phrases in the wrong
order—or he could have selected "medicines" unauthorized by
tradition, or omitted essential gestures. The other common excuse is that somebody else was on the scene first with strong
neutralizing or protective magic. Occasionally I have had individuals vindicating themselves with a statement that when officiating they must have been *bwasava*, a condition never
mentioned except in the context of abortive ritual effort.[11] A
person considers himself to be *bwasava*, I learned, when he feels
vague physical discomfort. Definitely he is not ill; but, equally
certain, he is not in perfect health. He aches but cannot point to
any painful limb or joint, discovers himself being irritable, avoids
companionship but hates being alone, and possibly has difficulty
in sleeping. There may or may not be a simple reason. He could
have been working hard and become overtired; or he could have
been chilled by prolonged exposure to cold, wet weather. Inevitably in these circumstances things go wrong. He sets out fishing
and leaves his hooks behind, breaks the handle of his axe, loses his
basket, picks areca nuts and drops them along the path, stubs his
toe, cuts himself, slips on the house ladder, and so on. What is
more natural than that his magic should miscarry? My reaction
was to enquire why nobody had told me of the condition at the
time. "We thought you'd know. Yes, magic always works, but
bwasava can be a complication," was the reply.

[11] *Bwasava* suggests a derivation from *bwasa*, "spell," but I could not find
support for my guess.

IX Religion and Social Structure

Perhaps the most striking feature of Wogeo society is a pervading duality. There is the split into moieties, the presence in each village of two headmen[1] and twin housing clusters, the pairing of the districts and their division into partners and adversaries, and the setting apart of the sexes. In a comprehensive view men and women are of nearly equal status; but their economic tasks, allegiances, rights, liabilities, and roles are all sharply contrasted.

The religious system reflects this dual framework. It seizes upon two distinct notions and, using them separately, cuts the world in the middle twice, as it were, both horizontally and vertically. The first set of halves it labels sacred and profane. Into the sacred go the culture heroes, ghosts, spirit monsters, and all that belong to such beings, including the awkward left hand and the uncomfortable cold; and into the profane goes the entire daily routine, as well as the right hand for working, and the cheerful warmth derived from spicy cooked meals, fire, and the sun. Contact between the halves is believed to be dangerous, and when such contact occurs steps have to be taken to avert disaster.

The second cut brings about the ritual separation of males and females, typified respectively by flutes and childbirth. The one is the source of pollution to the other, and again precautions are necessary to avoid the consequent hazards. Menstruation, natural and artificial, serves as the purifying agent, but in each case the patient must remain secluded for an appropriate interval.

[1]Two sets of two headmen, if we include besides the two headmen the man with the title "headman of the beach"—he who takes charge when the youths' tongues are scarified.

The moieties also appear directly in the shape of the ceremonial obligations that the members of each have towards those of the other. A person requires relatives belonging to the opposite group for his initiation, and, after he has died his family needs them for the burial. The debt thereby incurred is a heavy one, for initiators and those who perform mortuary ritual are drawn across the boundary between the profane and the sacred, and thus they become taboo and subject to unpleasant restrictions. It is a fact that sometimes the rule may be disregarded and the services of companions from the same moiety secured, but on such occasions the actors affirm what is correct by offering excuses.

Further structural elements are the local groups. Every naming ceremony gives formal acknowledgment of the uniformity of the traditions and culture, but the independence of the districts and villages is validated by a mythology that accounts for the minor differences of custom between them. Similarly, the specializations are backed up by the magical formulae peculiar to the units in question. The representation of the housing clusters in the religion again gives the lie to the native statement that the residents do not form a recognizable group. The culture heroes before their disappearance placed slabs of basalt in the ground near where they were living, and from the time of the ancestors on, a man's connection with a particular hero has given him the right to build his dwelling alongside the same being's stone. Hence the present clusters are derived directly from those established by the heroes.

The political organization goes hand in hand with religion. The headman calls up the various monsters from the spirit world, and he alone owns the dance masks and flutes that bring them to life. His followers may wish to have a feast or an initiation ceremony arranged, but the final decision rests with him. His social position is also underlined by his right to order the playing of the flutes when events of importance take place in the village or in his household—perhaps the construction of a new club or the coming of age of his daughter—and by the heads of the neighboring clusters sending their flutes to offer sympathy if he is overtaken by illness or some other misfortune.

Magic and Leadership

In all the societies of Melanesia specialists own numbers of the magical systems concerned with major enterprises. Such systems may include that for profitable trading voyages, that for winning battles, and that for securing bountiful harvests. Further, the fact of a man's knowing a system confers upon him the right to guide the practical aspects of the associated undertaking. Thus the canoe magician directs the trading expedition, the war magician is in charge of the raiding party, and the garden magician organizes horticulture.

The normal pattern of leadership for the region is by achievement rather than by ascription. The person who aims at rising to the top must so impress his fellows by the efforts he makes that they come to accept his superior claims. Generosity is the quality they admire most, and he gives away so much that they are all in his debt. Unable to repay him in kind, they discharge their obligations by deferring to him and showing him respect. A magical speciality is not essential to upwards progress, but an individual gains advantage over possible rivals if he happens to be one of the principal magicians.

Wogeo belongs to the minority of communities where headmen hold their position by virtue of birth. True, succession is not automatic, and an office holder must nominate his heir and sponsor him in a great ceremony (see above pp. 77-78, 93-94). Whoever is selected then receives instruction in the entire corpus of the local specialist magical systems. Thus each Wogeo headman has a virtual monopoly within his residential cluster of the magic relating to group tasks and group wellbeing. If his unit is one that engages in overseas trade, then he performs the rites for a successful expedition; should the people agree that a raid is to be made on some other place, he casts the spells for victory; when a festival is proposed, he is responsible for the ceremonies before the communal garden is planted; at the festival itself he chants the nodding spells to preserve harmony; he is supposed to be familiar with sorcery to kill offenders and with inquest ritual to detect its use by others; and, perhaps most important in the eyes of his followers, they can look to him to bring sunny weather. Accordingly he manages the trading voyages, has charge of the warriors in an attack, regulates collective gardening, superintends festivals, controls the practices of sorcery and divination, and is believed to have the power of stopping the all-too-prevalent rain. It is scarcely a matter of surprise that he should enjoy high status and great prestige.

Religion and Kinship

Commonly in Melanesia religion is closely linked also with the kinship system. If in ordinary life those belonging to each category of kinsfolk have to behave differently, then the chances are that varying ritual duties will be assigned to them. Where the paternal uncles treat their nephews in one way and the maternal uncles in another, for example, we may expect to see them taking up separate positions in ceremonies. The occasion above all when such kinship norms crystallize is the funeral. Tradition then lays down what part every class of relatives has to play. Doubtless many of those who attend are grief-stricken, but if so this is a private matter and, in the social sphere, irrelevant. It is decreed which persons must weep and to what extent, which sing dirges, which bury the body, which serve refreshments, and so on. Such a visible demonstation of the several relationship ties is the first move towards the reintegration of the society shattered by the death.

Wogeo confirms the rule despite the lack of precise distinctions between the conduct expected from the various kinds of relatives. Although a youth addresses his father's brothers as *mam* and his mother's brothers as *wawa*, he looks upon them as more or less equivalent; and they reciprocate by respectively speaking of him as *natu* and *kalawa* but behaving as though the bonds were of nearly identical quality. There is little, too, to permit the drawing of a line between the actions of cognates and affines; they are expected to be alike helpful and dependable. The religion follows the same principles and refrains from making discriminatory demands. Paternal uncles, maternal uncles, the other cognates, and the affines are ritually indistinguishable. All the kindred and all the in-laws are expected to go along to the funeral, and the only persons in any way marked off from the rest are those regarded as especially close. The heaviest responsibilities rest upon the parents, the uncles and aunts on both sides, the brothers and sisters, the cousins, the children, and the nephews and nieces; and none but they need remain for long with the corpse or actually handle it. Even the gravediggers are designated according to group affiliation rather than according to kinship ties. They must be of the opposite moiety, and whether they are paternal uncles, patrilateral or matrilateral cross cousins, sons or brothers' sons, or distantly related neighbors is of no concern to anyone. The approach to social reintegration is achieved by the very presence at the ceremonies of the widest circle of kinsfolk and marriage connections.

X   The Moral System

In the first chapter I said that Wogeo mythology provides ultimate validity for both the physical and the social universe. The mythology enshrines the dogma that the culture heroes created the natural environment and established a model for human conduct. Man is thus revealed as part of a plan drawn up before the beginning of time; if he follows the path laid down by the culture heroes, his life will achieve perfection. The moral system, in other words, is translated from the human to the supernatural plane. Some people may be aware that the community benefits when each member willingly fulfills the legitimate claims of his fellows, but the majority do not argue on grounds of expediency. They simply insist that the code of behavior has divine authority. Right is right because the culture heroes so decreed, and to criticize or question is tantamount to blasphemy.

As in other parts of the world, however, Satan may quote the scriptures for his own purpose. Thus householders guilty of some lapse have been known to justify their conduct by distorting the implications of a myth. When this kind of distortion occurs, other folk are quick to condemn the misinterpretation as casuistry. A close companion of mine once asked me to provide him with an alibi should the adulterous encounter he was about to undertake give rise to suspicion. On my reminding him that not long before he had deplored extramarital intrigues as wrong, he replied that reflection had led him to change his mind. "If the culture hero Wonka could commit adultery with the wife of his blood brother, why shouldn't I do so?" he concluded. Later I raised the matter as a talking point in the club, naturally without reference to any specific person. Those present chided me for being silly. Had I

193

forgotten that the husband, Mafofo, had punished his wife and her lover by setting fire to the house in which they were imprisoned? The pair may have escaped then, but in the end they were obliged to forsake their island home. Enforced exile is proof of adverse judgment (see above pp. 47-48).

The blanket backing for accepted morality has obviated the need for explicit supernatural sanctions for every particular rule. Only three rules receive this kind of support—those forbidding sexual relations inside the moiety, trespass, and adultery with the spouse of a near kinsman. There is good reason for the reinforcement. Pressure is brought to bear on offenders who otherwise would be difficult to detect. They are made to admit their fault, and blame can thus be assigned and the norms reaffirmed. Moiety incest, for example, unlike a breach of exogamy, which cannot possibly be concealed, might pass unheeded if one or the other of the pair fails to confess. The man has no fears, for he escapes punishment, but the girl could be faced with childbirth. Prolonged labor always gives rise to doubt about the woman's honesty, though if she appears to be dying and still protests her innocence people are satisfied that she must be a victim of black magic.

We have seen that the living heroes are thought to punish with illness anyone who enters territory where he has no right to be. The remedy for this kind of illness is easy. The victim tells the owners and begs them to make a sham sacrifice on his behalf. Once this is done his recovery can be confidently assumed. The point here is that an owner has no hope of policing his land boundaries, but when assured that a thief's conscience will soon receive a prod he can sit back content in the realization that any depredations will come to an end.

Confession is also the sensible course when someone has had intercourse with the spouse of a close relative, though escape is not quite so certain, and the couple continues to face the possibility of perishing from a painful disease. In this instance not only is publicity given to the actions of the offenders, but also relief is given to those who have been wronged. Kinsmen, especially close kinsmen, are taught that they must at all times be loyal to one another, and, in addition, that if by chance one of them does so far forget himself as to disregard his obligations, then in the interests of the general good the rest ought not to make a move against him—they should continue to behave as though unaware of his action. Hence the correct procedure for a householder who finds that his wife has been unfaithful with his cousin is to keep quiet and refrain from any kind of retaliation. In such circumstances the thought that the sin may still have to be paid for is a potential source of satisfaction. One positive move alone is open to the injured party: He can shame the culprits by the ostentatious destruction of some of his own property. A wronged husband of my acquaintance threw a flaming torch into the thatch of his house in an attempt to burn it down. He deliberately chose the moment when a crowd was present, and as it happened someone was able to climb up quickly and put the fire out before much damage was done.

Other supernatural sanctions operate but are bound up not with immoral conduct but with ritual infringements. As we saw, a person who is in a state of taboo, *rekareka*, must avoid contact with others, and they in turn must avoid contact with him or her. A menstruating woman is a lesser hazard to herself than to her companions, especially those of the opposite sex; but menstruating men, childbearing women, mourners, and the rest are a menace to everybody, themselves not excepted. The lightest touch means death, death for the one touching, death for the one touched, and accordingly they have to be shut out of public life.

Sanctions of this type have a direct bearing on the internal harmony of Wogeo society. In theory most deaths, except those of infants, are the result of sorcery, and if the topic is raised in open discussion, those present insist that we would all live until overtaken by physical decrepitude and mental dotage were it not for the malice of those skilled in black magic. But in practice the only time a considered accusation of sorcery can be taken for granted is after an important person has died. Such a man may have been widely suspected of adultery with the wife of a close relative, even a brother, or known to have been guilty of moiety incest, but at his demise the sins are ignored, and discussion centers exclusively on sorcery. The prestige of his kinsmen and affines demands that they have revenge. Yet they may still doubt the advisability of taking action openly against the individual supposed to have been responsible—the consequences of doing so could easily be disastrous—and sometimes they are content with their own counter-sorcery.

In practice, for an overwhelming majority of the deaths the reason accepted is a broken taboo. At first the immediate relatives may argue that the deceased must have been a sorcery victim, but ultimately they give in to popular opinion. They agree that perhaps after all he may have inadvertently brushed against a menstruating woman or that a menstruating woman may unawares have sat on his sleeping mat; or he could have been careless when last he incised his penis, or another man whose penis had not healed may have thoughtlessly offered him a cigarette. These are conjectures, and no method exists whereby the true cause might be ascertained. If the loss is in this way attributed to misadventure, then obviously vengeance need not be considered. Instead of the survivors having to identify and kill the enemy, thereby possibly starting a vendetta, they continue their normal relationships with everybody.

Thus, although Wogeo religion enables evil to be projected outwards away from the self and blame in consequence ascribed to known or imagined opponents, it has an escape clause offering what is usually in the end a more acceptable alternative—the doctrine that misfortune can also come about by sheer accident. Each person takes comfort from the knowledge that the woes he has to suffer are caused by the wickedness of those who hate him; and by the time his relatives have come to accept another explanation, one that will give them less trouble, he is dead and so past caring. The destructive effects if a feud were to develop every time an adult expires in his bed can be imagined. The total population of the island is less than a thousand, and the inevitable consolidation of small groups of kindred following on continuous warfare would soon lead to the erosion of social life and eventually to chaos.

Wogeo Bibliography

The works listed are all by I. Hogbin.

"Native Culture of Wogeo," *Oceania*, Vol. 5 (1934-1935), pp. 308-337.

"Trading Expeditions in Northern New Guinea," *Oceania*, Vol. 5 (1934-1935), pp. 375-407.

"Adoption in Wogeo," *Journal of the Polynesian Society*, Vol. 44 (1935), pp. 208-215 and Vol. 45 (1936), pp. 17-38.

"Sorcery and Administration," *Oceania*, Vol. 6 (1935-1936), pp. 1-32. A general study with some references to Wogeo.

"Mana," *Oceania*, Vol. 6 (1935-1936), pp. 241-274. A general study with some references to Wogeo.

"Social Reaction to Crime: Law and Morals in the Schouten Islands," *Journal of the Royal Anthropological Institute*, Vol. 68 (1938), pp. 223-262.

"Tillage and Collection," *Oceania*, Vol. 9 (1938-1939), pp. 127-151, 286-325. Reprinted in revised form in I. Hogbin and P. Lawrence, *Studies in New Guinea Land Tenure* (Sydney 1967).

"Native Land Tenure in New Guinea," *Oceania*, Vol. 10 (1939-1940), pp. 113-165. Reprinted in revised form in I. Hogbin and P. Lawrence, *Studies in New Guinea Land Tenure* (Sydney 1967).

"The Father Chooses His Heir: a Family Dispute over Succession in Wogeo," *Oceania*, Vol. 11 (1940-1941), pp. 1-40.

"A New Guinea Infancy: From Conception to Weaning in Wogeo," *Oceania*, Vol. 13 (1942-1943), pp. 285-309. Reprinted in revised form as "A New Guinea Childhood from Conception to the Eighth Year" in L. L. Langness and John C. Weschler, eds., *Melanesia: Readings on a Culture Area* (Scranton 1970).

"Marriage in Wogeo," *Oceania*, Vol. 15 (1944-1945), pp. 324-352.

"Puberty to Marriage: a Study of the Sexual Life of the Natives of Wogeo," *Oceania*, Vol. 16 (1945-1946), pp. 185-209.

"A New Guinea Childhood: From Weaning to the Eighth Year in Wogeo," *Oceania*, Vol. 16 (1945-1946), pp. 275-296. Reprinted in revised form as "A New Guinea Childhood from Conception to the Eighth Year" in L. L. Langness and John C. Weschler, eds., *Melanesia: Readings on a Culture Area* (Scranton 1970).

Peoples of the Southwest Pacific (New York 1945). Includes 33 photographs from Wogeo.

"Sorcery and Succession in Wogeo," *Oceania*, Vol. 23, (1952-1953), pp. 133-136.

"Wogeo Kinship Terminology," *Oceania*, Vol. 34 (1963-1964), pp. 208-209.

Social Change (Melbourne 1970). A general study with some references to Wogeo.

"Food Festivals and Politics in Wogeo," *Oceania*, Vol. 40 (1969-1970), in press.

Index

Administration. *See* Government
Adultery, 17, 26, 86, 89, 98-99, 146, 148, 195; and mythology, 42-49, 50, 193, 194
Affines, 22, 24, 25, 146, 156, 162, 167, 191, 192
Aged, death of, 142
Age grades, 102
Agnates, 19, 20, 22
Agriculture, 7, 15, 19, 21, 25, 35; and ritual, 85, 90, 175, 190, 191; and sorcery, 153
Allen, M. R., 86n.
Alliances, system of, 10, 11
Ancestors, 12, 57, 166, 177, 178
Arapesh, 96
Art, 77
Astronomy, and culture heroes, 30-31

Bemba, 98
Big man. *See* Headman
Birth, 91, 92, 137-140, 189, 194, 195
Blood, 85, 88, 92, 93, 94, 114-120, 164. *See also* Cold, Menstruation
Bond friend. *See* Brother
Bones, of ancestors, 12, 57, 166, 177, 178
Bride price, 86
Brother, blood, 45, 113, 123, 136, 152, 165, 193
Busama, 24n., 83n.

Calendar, 7
Calvesi, M., 49n.
Canoes, 14, 16, 25, 36, 43-51, 54, 59, 61, 91, 133n., 141, 145, 160, 177, 191. *See also* Trade

Caravaggio, M. M., 49n.
Ceremonial fight, 105, 109, 133, 134, 135, 136
Children, death of, 141, 142
Christian mission, 9
Christian sects, 49, 50
Clan, 25. *See also* Housing cluster
Clothing, 9, 65, 106, 107, 111, 120, 125, 149
Clubhouse, 14, 25, 46, 49, 50, 57, 61, 63, 67, 70, 72, 76, 77, 79, 80, 83, 89, 90, 93, 95, 105, 184, 189, 193; description of, 11, 12; and initiation, 101, 102, 106-114
Cluster. *See* Housing cluster
Codere, H., 79n.
Cold, ritual for driving away, 80, 81, 84, 85, 93, 94, 95, 117, 127, 128, 152, 158, 163, 164, 175, 180, 188, 190
Cooking. *See* Food
Cordyline, use in ritual of, 67n.
Crops. *See* Food
Culture heroes, 27-54, 78, 119, 168, 177, 186, 188, 193; and precedents, 28, 37, 46, 49, 50, 51, 53; and geography and astronomy, 30-31; and technology, 33, 34; and institutions, 34-38, 174, 175, 183, 184, 185, 193; and topography, 38-51; and stones, 14, 15, 48, 49, 51, 189; and disputed myths, 50, 51; living, 51-53, 141, 194; and sex relations, 100, 101, 110, 117. *See also* Mythology, Spirit monsters
Curry, recipe, 85

Dance, 63-68, 77, 131
Death, 144-152, 156-167, 195; by accident, 145, 149; of children, 141, 142; of aged, 142. See also Funeral
Descent, 18, 22, 25, 98. See Moiety
Diet. See Food
Dinka, 171, 172, 173
Disease. See Illness
Districts, 10
Dowry, 20, 73, 99
Douglas, M., 95-98, 171-173
Dracaena, 67n.
Drug plants. See Food

Ear piercing, 104–106
Elderly. See Aged
Enemies, system of, 10, 11
Enga, Mae, 96-98
Evans-Pritchard, E. E., 168
Exogamy, 17, 194. See also Marriage, Moiety

Festival. See Food
Fight, ceremonial, 105, 109, 133, 134, 135, 136
Filiation, 25
Firth, R., 6n.
Fishing, 12, 13, 16, 25, 33, 34, 35, 39, 66, 70, 112
Flute spirits (Nibek monsters), 12, 17, 58, 59, 66, 72, 73, 75, 76, 79, 80, 82, 93, 95, 100-124, 130, 136, 160, 189, 190
Folk tales, 28-30, 49
Food, 19, 65, 67, 70, 92, 100, 101, 104, 105, 106, 108, 124, 125, 128, 133, 175, 176; preparation of, 16, 129, 130; and mythology, 32, 33, 35, 36, 39, 40, 41, 42; emotional attitude to, 71; and taboo, 83, 84, 85, 89, 108, 114, 115, 116, 118, 156; and festivals, 58, 67, 70, 71, 72, 76-79, 94, 95, 125, 128, 133-135, and magic, 182, 191
Fortune, R. F., 6, 148n.
Frazer, J. G., 6, 171
Friend. See Brother
Fruit. See Food

Fumigation, ritual, 134
Funeral, 18, 33, 94, 95, 130, 138, 139, 146, 158-167, 189, 190, 192

Gardens. See Agriculture
Geography and culture heroes, 30-31
Genealogies, 22, 23
Ghosts, 37, 38, 55-57, 68, 80, 94, 95, 141, 142, 154, 155, 156, 159, 168, 189
Goody, J., 83n., 85n.
Government, 9, 147, 161n.
Guadalcanal, 82, 152

Headdress, 21-124
Headman, 17, 18, 19, 20, 21, 25, 33, 34, 39, 42, 48, 51, 58, 59, 61, 63, 66, 70, 72, 75, 76, 77, 79, 80, 93, 94, 95, 102, 104, 105, 108, 109, 113, 119, 130, 140, 153, 154, 188, 189; of the beach, 114, 188n.; and magic, 175-176, 189, 190, 191; and sorcery, 153, 154; and death, 160, 164, 165; and inquest, 154-156
Health. See Illness
Heat. See Cold
Homosexuality, 90
Horticulture. See Agriculture
House, description of, 12, 13, 35
Housing cluster, 18, 26, 59, 63, 66, 70, 95, 114, 143, 159, 165, 166, 188, 189, 190
Hunting, 13, 16, 36, 38, 52, 83, 91, 133n., 141
Husband. See Marriage

Illness, 53, 143, 144, 150, 156, 157, 170, 185, 186, 187, 189; reaction of patient, 142; treatment by magic, 91, 143, 146, 186, 187; and menstruation, 91, 142, 145, 150
Incest, 17, 90, 194, 195
Incision of penis. See Menstruation
Inheritance, 18, 19, 20, 21, 25, 34, 49, 73, 98, 114, 151, 152, 156, 168, 176, 190

Initiation, 72, 87, 88, 95, 100-124, 189; stages, 101, 102, 103; purpose, 103; ear piercing, 104-106; admission to club, 101, 102, 106-114; scarifying tongue, 114-120, 134; and stealing food, 115; and menstruation, 120, 121; and headdress, 120-124
Inquest, 144, 147, 148, 154-156, 191
Institutions and culture heroes, 34-38, 174, 175, 183, 184, 185, 193, 194
Instruments, musical, 73-75

Japanese, 9

Karok, 170n.
Kin, 17, 18, 36, 37, 61, 87, 105, 111, 113, 116, 121, 123, 124, 126, 128, 129, 130, 133, 138, 139, 144, 146, 182, 183; mutual responsibilities of, 13, 21-26, 143, 194, 195; terminology, 23, 24; and religion, 191, 192; and death, 156, 157-167
Kindred, 22, 191
Krige, J. D. and E. J., 85n.
Kroeber, L., 170n.

Labor, wage, 9, 90, 161
Land, rights to, 19-21, 25, 61-62, 141; and mythology, 51, 52, 53, 54, 190
Langness, L. L., 86n.
Lawrence, P., 6n., 7n., 19n., 26n., 62n., 71n., 93n.
Leenhardt, M., 67n.
Left hand, in ritual, 69, 81, 85, 89, 112, 113, 117, 134, 150, 151, 152, 163, 188
Legends, 28, 29
Lele, 96-98
Lewa. See Spirit monsters
Lienhardt, R. G., 173n.
Lineage, 25. See also Housing cluster

Mae Enga, 96-98
Magic, 18, 27, 43-45, 47, 49, 50, 51, 52, 54, 57, 75, 77, 78, 90, 94, 114, 116, 117, 118, 119, 120, 124, 129, 138, 140, 145, 166, 168; and mythology, 32, 34, 35, 36, 39, 40, 41; and cold, 85, 117; and agriculture, 85, 175; and property, 143, 185, 186, 187; and illness, 91, 143, 146, 186, 187; and headmen, 174-176, 189, 190, 191; and control, 169-171; terms for, 174; spell, 174, 176-187; types, 174, 175, 176; medicine, 178, 179, 180, 182-187; rite, 179-197; infallibility of, 186, 187; and food, 181, 182, 190
Malaita, 28, 82
Male cult, 100-124
Malinowski, B., 53n., 148n., 171, 172, 181
Mana, 171
Marigum, 11, 21, 49, 50, 68, 69, 70, 73, 74, 102, 107, 126, 130, 133, 146, 147, 148, 153, 154, 155, 166, 175, 176, 183, 184
Masks, 12, 62, 63, 70, 93, 189
Mead, M., 96n.
Meggitt, M. J., 6n., 86n., 96n.
Medicine, 178, 179, 180, 182-187. See also Illness
Men's house. See Clubhouse
Menstruation, 113, 118, 188, 195, 196; female, 86, 87, 88, 89, 102n., 136, 137, 145, 146, 189, 195, 196; a girl's first, 72, 89, 114, 125-136; male, 88, 89, 91, 92, 102n.; incising penis to induce, 88, 89, 102, 103, 121; a boy's first, 89, 114, 120, 121; frequency for men, 91; and success in secular affairs, 90; physical effects of on men, 91, 141; and illness, 91, 142, 145, 150
Mission, Christian, 9
Moiety, 17, 18, 22, 23, 26, 30, 85, 99, 104, 105, 108, 112, 113, 116, 119, 121, 122, 123, 133, 161, 188, 189, 192, 194, 195
Monsters. See Spirit monsters

Morals, and mythology, 29, 49, 53,
    193
Mozart, W. A., 73
Murder, 95, 105, 166, 167; and
    mythology, 36, 37, 38, 47,
    50
Music, effects of, 66; instruments,
    73-75
Mythology, 18, 28-54, 60, 78, 100,
    101, 103, 110, 111, 175, 176,
    177, 182, 183, 184, 186, 189,
    193, 194. See also Culture
    heroes, Spirit monsters

Nadel, S. F., 170n.
Nambudiri Brahmins, 98
Naming ceremony, 61, 63, 75, 77,
    78, 139, 190
Nibek. See Flutes, Spirit monsters
Nuer, 98, 168
Nuts. See Food

Oil, coconut, method of making,
    129, 130
Ornaments, 9, 17, 33, 36, 43, 52, 61,
    67, 68, 73, 94, 111, 112, 119,
    120, 129, 131, 157, 159, 160,
    162, 165, 183, 184, 185
Ownership. See Land

Painting. See Art
Palolo worm, 90, 93, 147
Penis, incision of. See Menstruation
Physical type, 9
Physiology, theories of, 180
Pigs, 16, 24, 52, 58, 65, 72, 76, 77,
    78, 80, 83, 91, 94, 105, 106,
    107, 108, 109, 112, 124, 160,
    165
Polygamy, 13, 18, 37, 38
Population, 7, 9, 10
Pots, 13, 16, 51. See also Trade
Property, and magic, 143, 186, 187;
    See also Land
Profane and sacred, 82, 83, 94, 95,
    188, 189, 195

Raiding. See Warfare
Rainbow snakes, 52
Rekareka. See Taboo

Residence, pattern of, 19, 20, 21.
    See also Housing cluster
Revenge. See Vengeance
Right hand. See Left hand
Ritual, and agriculture, 85, 90, 175,
    190, 191; for driving away
    cold, 80, 81, 84, 85, 93, 94, 95,
    117, 127, 128, 152, 158, 163,
    164, 175, 180, 188, 190; and
    fumigation, 134; use of cor-
    dyline in, 67n. See also Left
    hand

Sacred, and profane, 82, 83, 94, 95,
    188, 189, 195
Sahlins, M. D., 18n.
Scarifying the tongue, 114-120
Sculpture. See Art
Seligman, C. G., 148n.
Sepik River, 7
Sex, before marriage, 17; in ritual,
    86-92; women's status, 86, 98,
    99, 188; and illness, 83, 87, 89,
    91; attitude to sexual inter-
    course, 89, 90; flutes and, 100,
    101, 120; and boys' initiation,
    114-120; and girls' menstrua-
    tion, 126, 131, 133, 135; cul-
    ture heroes and, 100, 101, 110,
    117
Sexes, relations between, 34-38, 72,
    93, 95-99, 106, 108, 114, 125;
    women imitate men's cere-
    monies, 131, 135. See also
    Menstruation, Taboo
Sickness. See Illness, Death
Snakes, rainbow, 52
Social structure, 17-26
Sorcery, 53, 57, 90, 142, 191, 195,
    196; preventing quarrels, 143,
    144, 170; and illness, 143, 144,
    170; training sorcerer, 151,
    152; precautions against, 152;
    and sexual intercourse, 152;
    and death, 143, 144, 145, 146,
    147, 148-154, 194; and head-
    men, 153, 154; to spoil gar-
    dens, 153, 154
Soul. See Ghosts
Spells, 174, 176-187

Spirit monsters, 48-81, 82, 130, 168,
   188, 189; *lewa* (*tangbwal*),
   58-71, 131; *mbek*, 71-81, 100-
   124; summoning, 60, 61, 75,
   76, 94, 95; dismissing, 67-69,
   79-81, 94, 95; and women, 72.
   See also Culture heroes
Stealing, 115
Succession, 18, 78, 94, 98, 191
Stones, and culture heroes, 14, 15,
   48, 49, 51, 189
Suicide, 87
Symbols, 171, 172, 173

Taboo, 29, 43, 63, 65, 70, 75, 82-124,
   127, 128, 133, 148, 182, 189,
   195, 196; condition of, 83, 84;
   terminating, 85, 86; and sexual relations, 82-94; and spirits, 94, 95; and menstruation,
   136, 137; and birth, 137-140;
   and death, 158-167. *See also*
   Menstruation
Tangbwal. See Spirit monsters
Technology, and culture heroes, 33,
   34
Tongue, scarifying of, 114-120
Topography, and culture heroes,
   38-51
Trade, 16, 17, 28, 34, 57, 73, 91, 108,

121n., 141, 145, 166, 174, 175,
   177, 183, 184, 190, 191; and
   mythology, 42-51
Trespass, 53, 142, 194
Turner, V. W., 172n.

Unclean. *See* Sacred

Valuables. *See* Ornaments
Vatican, 49n.
Vengeance, 57, 143, 145, 146, 154,
   196
Village, population of, 10; description of, 11-15; plan of, 19, 21;
   harmony of, and magic, 143,
   144, 182, 190

Wage labor, 9, 90, 161
Walbiri aborigines, 96
Warfare, 9, 57, 91, 94, 95, 141, 166,
   167, 189, 190, 196; and myth-
   ology, 47
Wealth. *See* Ornaments, Property
Wife. *See* Marriage, Sexes
Witchcraft. *See* Sorcery
Women. *See* Sexes
Worm, palalo, 90, 93, 147

Yabou. See Sorcery
Yurok, 98, 170n.